TEXT AND REALITY
Aspects of Reference
in Biblical Texts

Bernard C. Lategan
and
Willem S. Vorster

FORTRESS PRESS
Philadelphia, Pennsylvania

SCHOLARS PRESS
Atlanta, Georgia

THE SOCIETY OF BIBLICAL LITERATURE
SEMEIA STUDIES

Lou H. Silberman, Editor

© 1985
The Society of Biblical Literature

Library of Congress Cataloging in Publication Data

Lategan, Bernard C.
  Text and reality.

  (Semeia studies)
  Bibliography: p.
  1. Bible—Hermeneutics—Addresses, essays, lectures.
  2. Bible—Criticism, interpretation, etc.—Addresses,
  essays, lectures. I. Vorster, Willem S. II. Title.
  III. Series.
  BS476.L35   1985   220.6′01   85–47735
  ISBN 0-8006-1514-X (Fortress Press pbk. : alk. paper)
  ISBN 0-89130-823-7 (Scholars Press : pbk. alk. paper)

1774F85   Printed in the United States of America   1–1514
on acid-free paper

CONTENTS

Preface

The relationship between text and reality, between the "world" created by a written text and the "real" world as it exists outside of the text, has been a focal point in literary discussions since Aristotle introduced his famous concept of *mimesis*. In the case of biblical texts, the issue is even more acute. These texts do not only refer to specific events in history, but claim that the message they carry is indissolubly bound up with the course of history.

What is the relationship between what actually happened and the way in which it is presented in the text? This is the classical formulation of the question from a historical perspective which gave rise to the emergence of the historical method—a method which has dominated theological thinking for many decades.

Recent developments in literary theory have opened up new perspectives in this field. At the same time, the perception of the problem also changed. The emphasis has shifted from congruence to reference. The question is no longer: to what extent is there congruence between text and reality, but rather: in what way does the text refer to reality?

The four essays presented here explore some of the possibilities opened up by recent developments in literary theory. The focus is on biblical material and theoretical points are illustrated as far as possible with examples drawn from these texts. Two basic assumptions underlie the discussion: reference can only be considered adequately within the framework of a broader hermeneutical theory, and reference may offer a more satisfactory approach to the problem of history in biblical texts.

The first two essays were originally presented as papers at the meetings of the *Studiorium Novi Testamenti Societas* in Rome (1981) and Louvain (1982). The last two are the result of subsequent discussions between the authors and colleagues in which the relationship between reference and reception became more prominent. The fact that much of what is written here is presented in the style of tentative explorations, rather than final pronouncements, reflects the experimental nature of the studies and should be interpreted by the reader as an invitation to participate in the ongoing dialogue.

Bernard C. Lategan

Willem S. Vorster

1

Some Unresolved Methodological Issues in New Testament Hermeneutics

Bernard C. Lategan

Introduction

There can be little doubt that New Testament hermeneutics is moving through one of the most interesting phases of its development. This is evident from the continuing flow of new publications on the subject and the interest which the work of text theorists (and pragmatists!) enjoys at present. We find ourselves in the aftermath of an intense struggle between the historical method and the structuralist approach to the interpretation of biblical texts—a struggle which is not confined to theology, but has indeed a much wider scope. To mention one example from literary criticism, in the *Times Literary Supplement* of February 6, 1981, a report was published on the current debate within the English faculty of Cambridge University—which by now has spread outwards—on the question of how literature should be taught. Underlying the debate is a sharp division between those who defend the more "traditional" approach to texts and those who want to experiment with various other readings, especially those cast in a structuralist mold. It might be a comfort to theologians that colleagues in related disciplines are struggling with the same issues, but this does not necessarily help towards the solution of specific problems posed by the interpretation of biblical material.

Let us confine ourselves therefore to the field of biblical hermeneutics. The debate between the historical and structuralist approach has had, among others, the important consequence that it has sharpened the methodological issues at stake and that it has heightened our awareness of the role played by philosophical categories in the formulation of exegetical theory (cf. Thiselton, 1980:

3-10). The interpretation of texts of whatever kind is an activity which by its very nature involves a framework of systematic thought, be it on a conscious or subconscious level. It was this very focus on systematic presuppositions which made a certain degree of understanding or at least tolerance between the historical and structuralist positions possible. In fact, nowadays there is hardly a historical exponent who does not show awareness of structural problems or a structuralist who does not acknowledge the importance of the historical aspects of texts. An interesting example is the work developed under the direction of Daniel Patte. In an introductory essay to a recent publication of the group, Patte insists that the ultimate aim of structural exegesis is to serve the meaning-effect of the text, to proceed to a "theopoetic," prolonging the biblical text and respecting its mystery (Patte, 1980:22). He shows that two main types of structural exegesis are emerging, one of which is focused on the characteristics of the literary communication process, thereby inevitably having to face up to the historical aspects of understanding. Hans Dieter Betz's new commentary on Galatians may serve as an example at the other end of the spectrum. Working consciously within the historical-critical approach, Betz (1979) nonetheless gives a very detailed analysis of the epistle as an example of an apologetic letter, conforming to Hellenistic literary conventions. Of course, expertise in literary forms has always been part of the make-up of scholars working within this tradition, but in his awareness of the importance of structure, Betz is in fact addressing the same issues as his structuralist colleagues. Examples of a similar nature would not be difficult to find. More and more we are reading about the necessity to combine the historical and structural perspectives within a unifying methodological framework, and various attempts in this direction have already been made (cf. Beardslee, 1970; Crossan, 1979:1; Frey, 1970:35–40; Hartlich, 1980:12; McKnight, 1978:242; Ricoeur, 1973:201–21; Thiselton, 1980:440–41).

However, the present mood, favoring a peaceful co-existence and even an integration between the historical and structural approaches in the field of biblical exegesis, may be misleading. The intention behind this mood is no doubt commendable and most exegetes would surely welcome such a development. But unless some basic issues underlying the debate are successfully resolved, the danger exists that in the end exegetes would still make an exclusive choice, opting for either the historical or the structural paradigm, leading in some cases to a methodological stalemate and even a breakdown in scholarly communication.

It is my intention to focus on some of these underlying methodological issues, especially the relation between structure and history, the reception and transmission of the text, and the problem of reference. Before doing so, a few remarks regarding the status and function of written texts, in our case biblical texts, are called for. The influence of either the historical or the structural paradigm is so pervasive on the interpreter that the phenomenon of the text as such is seldom given adequate attention. We intend to take this phenomenon as our point of departure—not because we are under the illusion that this will safeguard us from facing the difficult questions already on the agenda or that our understanding of the text can ever be free from philosophical presuppositions. Rather, it is by concentrating on the features of the text itself that we may regain an understanding of the elements for which an adequate interpretation theory must provide and, by doing so, find a fresh entrance to the problems stated above.

In the case of biblical material the text exhibits three closely related features, namely, a *historical*, a *structural*, and a *theological* aspect.

By *historical* aspect it is meant that the text is historical in a two-fold sense: it is a historical phenomenon as such, with its own history which can be studied with historical methods; but at the same time it also refers to specific historical events in the past, for example, the life and crucifixion of Jesus and the proclamation of his death and resurrection by the early church.

By *structural* aspect it is meant that we encounter the text in the form of a specific structure, once again in a twofold sense: as a linguistic utterance it exhibits certain grammatical, syntactical, and semantic features and adheres to the rules of a specific code. But also the individual utterances themselves stand in a specific relation to one another, to the text as a whole, or the entire oeuvre of an author. On both these levels the structural relations can be described and systematized.

By *theological* aspect it is meant that biblical texts contain statements about God and man with specific soteriological and theological implications. Whether the interpreter identifies with these implications or not, the nature of the text—or to put it differently, the language game being played here—must be acknowledged and respected if an adequate inerpretation is the aim.

An important goal for theological hermeneutics at this stage is to deepen its understanding of the phenomenon of the text and to gain as clear an insight as possible into the interrelatedness of the three aspects mentioned above. It must be remembered that they never function in isolation or *in abstracto*, but as part of a dynamic process of communication. The text is in a certain sense the product of this process, but at the same time constructed with a view to mediate further understanding. Various models have been proposed to explain the communication process. We need not enter into a detailed discussion of the different proposals (cf. Dressler, 1973:92; Eco, 1972:166; Güttgemanns, 1978:14–18; Rossouw, 1980:17–26). Suffice to say that an important advantage of mapping out the course of textual communication in this way is that the various elements can be visualized in their relation to the process as a whole and that any one stage of the process can be brought into focus more sharply. For our purposes, the basic model developed by Roman Jakobson (1960:350–77), in which he distinguishes between six factors in linguistic communication (speaker, hearer, medium, code, situation, and message) and correlates them to six functions of language (emotive, conative, phatic, meta-linguistic, referential, and poetic), can serve as a general frame of reference, especially since its concept of communication as an interaction between a sender and a receiver via an intersubjective code or sign has been adopted by most other theories, including those developed for use with biblical material (cf. Güttgemanns, 1971b:225–30; Ricoeur, 1976:15, 26–44).

Within the general framework of a communication theory, we can now say something more with regard to the status of the written text as vehicle of understanding. The transition from the spoken to the written word has often been understood as a negative development. The argument runs as follows: the immediacy of personal contact is lost, the text inevitably is a drastic reduction of all the elements present in a situation of live communication. It is therefore an inadequate and often false representation of what has happened and what was understood in the original event. The text no doubt may appear at times to be a very thin and fragile thread to hold past and present together, to mediate understanding between original writer and modern reader. But inscripturation also has some important positive aspects which in fact make communication possible despite distance in time and space. The detachment from the original speaker-hearer situation by means of inscripturation need not imply a loss. It should rather be understood as a liberating move, which preserves the meaning of the event in a network of linguistic symbols and sets it free to reach a much wider audience. Because of the text, understanding is no longer a private affair restricted to certain individuals, but is brought into the open. As the text is *published*, in the full sense of the word, it becomes accessible to numerous potential readers. Although developed within a different context, this is exactly the force of Wittgenstein's argument against the concept of private language and his plea for public criteria of meaning (cf. Thiselton, 1980:379–82, and also Japp, 1977:51). The rules of the (language) game are known to its participants, and it is by adhering to a common code that communication becomes possible.

In its published form, the text begins a life of its own which the original author no longer controls—he can in fact become, as has been pointed out, his own reader. The relative semantic autonomy of the text (cf. Ricoeur, 1976:30) is important for the preservation of its message, as we shall presently see. At the same time, temporal and cultural distance from the original author opens the way to a multiplicity of readings of the same text and calls attention to the role of the reader in establishing the meaning of the text. The reception of the text is one of the problematic issues we shall be discussing at a later stage. At this point we only want to stress that the plurality of readings immediately raises the possiblity of misunderstanding and therefore also the question of a correct, or at least adequate, reading of the text—bringing us back to the basic theme of hermeneutics. In this respect the structure of the text performs a very important function, drawing the boundaries of possible interpretations and eliminating readings without an adequate foothold in the text itself. As Patte (1980:6) indicates, the text will remain hopelessly ambiguous without the selecting process performed by the network of relations which constitutes it.

Structure and History

Against this background, we can now turn to specific unresolved methodological issues. The first concerns the relation between history and structure in the text. By taking the written text as our focal point, we are deliberately confining ourselves to *one* form of language usage. We are aware that the word "language" is used to describe phenomena of communication on a variety of levels—language as a syntactic-semantic device, language as a medium of understanding (cf. the idea of *Sprachereignis*), or language as an ontological concept (cf. the work of Heidegger). The different levels on which language operates form the background of our remarks about history and structure and we shall occasionally refer back to them.

It has already been mentioned that currently there is a virtual consensus among exegetes that both the structural and historical aspects of the biblical text must be adequately accounted for in any successful hermeneutical theory. To quote McKnight:

> Structural analysis cannot be done apart from historical and existential consideration. In summary, the reader cannot discern elements and structures of meaning apart from the particular manifestation of those elements and structures to other particular historical phenomena. (1978:250–51)

Crossan (1979:1) writes about the present situation in biblical studies and "the growing conviction that the complete analysis of a biblical text demands both diachronic and genetic study of its causes and effects as well as synchronic and systemic study of its thematic or generic parallels." The problem is that the theoretical basis for the desired integration of structural and historical elements is seldom if ever clarified or even addressed.

The point that will be argued here is that the tension between structure and history on the level of the text is not the result of a clash between the structural and historical paradigms as theoretical conceptualizations, but that it finds its basis in the nature of the text itself. To find suitable categories to describe the nature of the text is not so easy, because the text combines within itself a dynamic and a static element—it is part of a process, but at the same time the suspension of that process. The contrast between the systematic and the historical perspective has been transposed on different levels into various antithetical pairs, for example: rule and experience, thought and life, essence and existence, the systematic and genetic, the constant and dynamic, *Notwendigkeit* and *Kontingenz*, synchrony and diachrony, to name just a few (cf. Visagie, 1978:46).

To describe the relationship between the historical and structural dimension of a written text, we first have to clarify what is meant by "historical" in this context. We have already said that the biblical text is historical in a twofold sense: it is a historical phenomenon in its own right, but it also refers to specific historical events in the past to which it claims to be a witness of some kind. This brings us to the knotty question of what in fact constitutes "history." Philosophers of history have pointed out that history is not based on the principle of completeness (giving *all* the facts), but rather on the principle of *selection*—John 20:30–31 expresses the same idea. Furthermore, history can never be merely the *bruta facta*, but in the narration of events a certain measure of interpretation is already implied. Not to acknowledge this means to disturb the fabric of history. Jüngel once made the cryptic remark: "Geschichtsforschung ist zugleich Geschichtsfälschung." History implies a structuring activity of some kind. What we see here is the problem of "Vertextung," which is a major theme in recent discussions in the field of historiography. Stempel (1973:325–46) shows that the issue is even more acute in history than in literary criticism. Whereas the latter by and large deals with texts already in existence, the former in most cases has to produce texts first of all. The form in which the historiographer presents his material involves a choice between various possibilities. The most usual form is the narration of events in some kind of sequential framework based on natural chronology. For example: *veni vidi vici*. Although a certain measure of flashback or anticipation is used, chronological order forms the backbone of narration. In the words of Reinhart Kosselleck: "Erst ein Minimum von Vorher und Nachher konstituiert die Sinneinheit, die aus Begebenheiten ein Ereignis macht" (1973:561). Over against this traditional form of historiography and under the influence of new developments in *sozialgeschichtliche* research, a new form of historiography has emerged, the so-called "Strukturgeschichte." By this is meant an account expressed not so much in terms of the succession of separate events, but in terms of categories of a certain duration, embracing longer periods of time. Typical examples of "structures" thus described would be: constitutional models, forms of government, production forces, social organization, and so on. The accent is on conditions or situations and, when applied to a longer period of time, is not unrelated to the well-known concept of "the spirit of the age"—which in itself is problematic and imprecise.

The differentiation between "history of events" (*Ereignisge-schichte*) and "history of structure" (*Strukturgeschichte*) gives rise to the further thesis that events can only be narrated, structures only described.[1] Whatever the merit of this thesis—and there are no doubt good arguments to support it—the point that interests us here is the *interrelatedness* of the two types of historiography. Separate events can only be identified as such against the backdrop of a wider framework or structure. Only when measured against a larger and relatively rigid scale do their specific features stand out and so arises the possibility of determining their "significance." To be recognized as an event and to function as such is therefore to be dependent on specific structural preconditions. Conversely, structures are built on what are perceived as concrete events and on the patterns they are thought to exhibit in their internal relations, their regularities or irregularities and their statistical data. It is in this context that Koselleck (1973:564) talks about the event as "Voraussetzung struktureler Aussagen." In his attempt to develop a general theory of narrative discourse, Ricoeur (1978a:183–84) is in fact addressing the same problem. He examines both historical and fictional narrative and argues that all narratives combine two dimensions in various proportions: the chronological or episodic (what we have called the historical) and the non-chronological or configurational (i.e., structural) dimensions. The telling of the story does not consist of piling one episode on top of the other, but also in construing significant wholes out of scattered events.[2] "The art of telling and, accordingly its counterpart, the art of following the story requires that we be able to elicit a configuration from a succession" (Ricoeur, 1978a:184). History, by definition, relies on a structuring operation.

The structuredness of history, however, is only one side of

---

[1] "Um meine These vorwegzunehmen: in der Praxis lässt sich eine Grenze zwischen Erzählung und Beschreibung nicht einhalten, in der Theorie histor-ischer Zeiten aber lassen sich die Ebene verschiedener zeitlicher Erstreckung nicht gänzlich aufeinander beziehen. Zur Verdeutlichung dieser These gehe ich zunächst—mit W-D. Stempel—davon aus, dass 'Ereignisse' nur erzählt, 'Struk-turen' nur beschrieben werden können" (Koselleck, 1973:560).

[2] For the wider aspects of "significance" (*Sinn*) in texts, cf. Enzensberger, 1981:44–60; Japp, 1977:46–48.

the coin. The discovery of the important role played by structure in verbal communication has led to the concept of the autosemantic nature of written texts. The text is seen as a self-contained entity, which in the first place should be analyzed and understood in terms of its internal relations and structure. The stress on text-immanent exegesis was motivated by a desire to take the text as text seriously and to exclude any considerations foreign to the text which might obscure its real meaning. This approach has much to commend itself and significant results have already been obtained. Nonetheless, it is important to realize that the autonomy of the text is a relative one. As a linguistic structure it inevitably has a specific *Woher* and *Wohin*, a distinctive setting as part of a wider process of communication. Indeed, the permanency of the internal relations of the text may be misleading. Although the formal relations between the various elements are unalterable, the value attached to these elements may differ from situation to situation. This is also the point behind Wittgenstein's insistence on the close connection between language and life and on the fact that when language-games change, there is a change in concepts and with the concepts, a change in the meaning of words. In the words of Thiselton (1980:375): "Indeed what speaking *is*, and what meaning *is*, depends on the surroundings in which language is being spoken." Although the text may resemble the freezing of the action in a film sequence on the screen, it is in fact always part of a wider movement of communication. Patte (1980:4) makes the same point when he shows that the relationship between text and reader is constantly changing, each time involving a different "hermeneutical circle." We have to accept therefore the *Geschichtlichkeit* of the structure of the text itself—or, to put it differently, its process-like nature. Both history and structure form part of the wider movement of the text in the process of communication and the interaction between these two elements is an important factor in maintaining this movement. This understanding of the relationship between history and structure also has implications for the referential function of the text, which will be considered in Chapter 3. We shall also not enter here into the intriguing question of the ontological basis for these epistemological or "communicative" observations and whether the text can be linked to basic traits of human experience, as Ricoeur (1978a:195) would argue. We only want to draw the methodological conclusion that if the historical and structural elements in biblical texts are seen in terms of a clash between the historical and structural paradigms, and if this is interpreted as necessitating an exclusive choice for either one of these paradigms, we are indeed heading for a hermeneutical cul-de-sac. If we accept, on the other hand, these two aspects as essential elements constituting the text as text and by whose dynamic interaction the communicative movement of the text becomes possible in the first place, we may have taken a small but important step towards the development of an adequate hermeneutics for biblical texts.

Reception and Transmission of the Text

The second methodological issue to be discussed here concerns the *reception* of the text. What happens at the receiving end of the communication process and what role does the reader play in determining the meaning of the text? In the field of literary history the phenomenon of reception recently has been the subject of intense discussion and has led, inter alia, to the development of an aesthetics of reception. This is designed to overcome the shortcomings of historical objectivism and to provide a new basis on which literary history can be rewritten (cf. Jauss, 1974a:11–41). A very important element in the theory is the "horizon of expectations" (*Erwartungshorizont*) with which the reader approaches the text. This approach gives rise to further questions, such as: Can we talk of the existence of a text apart from the reception by its readers? Does a text have one or several possible meanings? Japp sees as "das eigentliche Skandalon der modernen Hermeneutik" (1977:47) that we are faced with a choice between a hermeneutics of reduction, based on the assumption that the text has only one correct meaning, and a hermeneutics of unfolding (*Entfaltung*), opening up the richness of the text in terms of its polysemantic possibilities. Stated in different terms: Can a methodological distinction between explanation (presupposing uniformity) and application (presupposing multiplicity of meaning) be maintained? Furthermore, how does a specific interpretation influence subsequent readings of the text?

The role of the receptor of the text has always been an important issue in biblical hermeneutics insofar as it concerns the *completion* of the process of understanding. Since Dilthey this has been the counterpoint in all reflection on the hermeneutical process. In Gadamer's concept of the two horizons which merge when understanding takes place, the first is the horizon of the text, the latter that of the reader. In a similar way, Palmer (1969:24) insists that meaning is a matter of context, that an object does not have significance outside a relationship to someone, and that the relationship determines the significance. Explanation therefore is contextual or "horizonal." In most models of communication the receptor occupies a position of equal "status" as compared to that of the sender. Bartholomäus (1974:40–47), for instance, makes provision not only for the image which the sender has of the receptor but also for the expectations which the latter has of the sender. At the same time the individual and sociocultural position of the receptor is taken into account. The way in which Bultmann has developed the concept of *Vorverständnis*, and Fuchs's insistence that the text will only speak when the right questions are addressed to it, are indications of how seriously the role of the reader is taken in current biblical hermeneutics. Exponents of the New Hermeneutic, interpreting with a view to prepare a new *Sprachereignis*, would find little difficulty in identifying with Valéry's dictum that the "execution" of the poem is in fact the real poem (cf. Jauss, 1974a:14, n. 6). In fact, biblical hermeneutics has conceded the limits of formal explanation and accepts that the final event of understanding is an individual appropriation of the meaning of the text which can neither be regimented nor formalized.

It is not surprising, therefore, that in his development of an aesthetics of reception and impact, Jauss shows his indebtedness to the work of Gadamer. This becomes evident, for example, in the way a specialized *Rezeptionsgeschichte* is modeled on Gadamer's more general concept of *Wirkungsgeschichte*. Jauss himself intends to go even further by formalizing the constitutive elements in the process of reception—for example, the horizon of expectations brought to the text by contemporary and later readers. The aim of this operation is to develop a systematic approach to the phenomenon of reception and to provide the basis for a new methodological approach to literary criticism (Jauss, 1974a:25–27; Japp, 1977:51).

That the methodological aspects of reception call for further clarification is no doubt true. Schmidt (1975:399–408) has shown how the phenomenon of reception can be formalized to form part of an empirical working theory of literary communication for use in the field of *Literaturwissenschaft*. But Jauss intends to use reception also in a different way. He maintains that the aesthetic impact made by a specific text on contemporary and successive readers can serve as a criterion to determine the value and meaning of such a work. By doing so, he raises the interesting problem of the rise and fall of specific authors or literary works in different periods of time, and the question of whether the "success" of a work can be measured in this way. But once reception is used as a criterion for evaluating a specific text or is considered to be the dominant factor in determining its meaning, we encounter problems on both the empirical and theoretical level.

On the empirical level, reception can only be brought into consideration when it is *available*, that is, where the impact made by the work on its readers is adequately documented. Even where independent information of this kind is available, the status of such data is a problem on its own. This relates to questions such as who qualifies as sample readers (literary critics, the "average reader," the public at large), what are dependable indicators of acceptance (volume of sales, period of popularity), whether every text has a natural or implicit reader, and so on. Methodologically speaking, the theory of reception at this point finds itself in the same dilemma as the historical-critical approach in biblical exegesis, where the usefulness of the method is in direct relation to the data available. Where independent or supplementary data is lacking, we are thrown back on the information available in the text itself. There are special cases where the reception of the text has been documented in a subsequent reinterpretation of the text, and we shall shortly be looking at some examples in biblical literature, but these are exceptions to the rule.

On the theoretical level, the exact input of reception and its relationship to other components in the process of literary communication—for example, text-production and text-mediation (to use Schmidt's terminology)—becomes an issue (1975:403). Work in this field has made it clear that the idea of one, "correct" reading of the text is an illusion and that any hermeneutical theory must account for the polysemantic nature of texts. This implies a choice against a "Hermeneutik der Reduktion" and for a "Hermeneutik der Entfaltung" (cf. Japp, 1977:47), and the recognition of the "open-ended" nature of the text. The acceptance of the multiplicity of possible readings does not put paid to the question of validity, but rather makes it more acute. This calls for the methodological strengthening and expansion of the reception side of our interpretation theory. To quote Schmidt in this respect:

> In order to explain the possible roles a literary text may play, a theory of literary communication needs of course an explicit text-semantics. This text-semantics must be able to specify under what conditions and in relation to what groups of readers certain texts can be assigned certain interpretations (in the logical sense of the word). But this procedure is only one part of a new concept of interpretation seen as a theory complementary to a theory of literary communication. The full task of this complementary theory is to specify the relations between all components of the process of literary communication (author, text, editor, media, readers, critics, scholars, etc.) with regard to an *individual* text or a closed set of texts. (1975:403–4)

What is needed therefore, is the broadening of the theoretical base to accommodate the aspects of reception in such a way that its inter-relatedness with text-production and text-mediation becomes clear. To concentrate all attention on the act of reception, thereby making the reader the almost exclusive arbiter over, or creator of, the meaning of the text, not only overextends the contribution reception has to make but also foreshortens the process of understanding in a dangerous way. All the problems associated with the concept of "intentional fallacy" could thus be repeated in the form of a "receptor's fallacy." The question of validity is not concerned with prescribing one exclusive meaning-possibility to a text, but rather with drawing the boundaries within which the process of successful understanding is to take place. It accepts that understanding is a *mediating* process in which the text is a vehicle, serving as an *Umweg* to make communication in a new set of circumstances possible. The text contains explicit formal constraints and definite signals which are to be honored if we agree to take its intention seriously. These indicators are to be found on various levels of the text—for example, the level of the grammatical-syntactic structure, that of the genre, and that of the macro-text as such.

Together these indicators form a network of relations which not only sets the outer limits of the possibilities of interpretation, but at the same time points out the direction the interpretation is intended to follow—bringing the *Selbstverständnis* of the reader under critical scrutiny and proposing an alternative understanding of himself and the world in which he finds himself. The text with its constraints thus serves as the *Gegenüber* or foil, which is not only interpreted by the reader but which, in its turn, interprets and shapes the reader.

The final act of understanding is indeed an existential event, implying an individual and personal decision regarding the meaning of the text. It cannot be manipulated or controlled and the limits of what can be achieved by the scaffolding of theory must be accepted. The preparation for the act of understanding and the reflection upon it—giving reasons for a specific reading—no longer is a private affair, but must be able to stand up to public scrutiny, to be justified in terms of the text and the situation of the receptor. If a theory of reception excludes this intersubjective dimension of understanding from its field of vision, the issue of misunderstanding also ceases to be a problem, because the possibility of an invalid reading is theoretically denied. But then it may be asked if, under these circumstances, meaningful communication through the medium of texts is still a practical possibility.

At this point an important distinction should be kept in mind. The question of a "valid" reading is closely tied to the *type* of text under consideration. The problem of an adequate/ inadequate reading becomes more acute in the case of "normative" texts, like religious and legal literature. Here the pressure towards conformity is indeed stronger than in literary texts of a less committed nature. Added to this is the influence of the body of believers which in theological thought is the *Ort* where understanding takes place. This represents a special form of the insistence on public criteria for interpretation and makes understanding even more of a communal matter. But even here, the intention of communicative participation in the process of interpretation is not to close off the text in a rigid stereotyped reading, but rather to make sure that it is launched on its proper trajectory, thereby keeping it open to its intended future.

In concluding this section, let us consider a specific example in biblical literature where the reception of a text has been recorded and included in a subsequent re-interpretation of the text—a phenomenon which we shall call the "enriched text" and which only occurs in literature with a relatively long history. According to Matt 12:3–4, Jesus in his dialogue with the Pharisees refers to David who in his flight from Saul went into the house of God and took the consecrated loaves—an act forbidden by the law of Moses. In its present setting this episode is in fact the record of a threefold reception telescoped into one text: David's reading of the Mosaic law in the specific circumstances of his flight, Jesus' reading of this already enriched text (combining the Mosaic law and David's reading of it), and Matthew's use of Jesus' reading to fulfill a specific function in the macrostructure of his gospel aimed at his original readers. Eventually also the present reader adds his own horizon as a further dimension to the text. The phenomenon of the enriched text ties in with a series of related issues concerning the use of the Old Testament in the New, the effect of ongoing history on the understanding of past events, the verification of historical statements, and so on. Hans Weder (1980:64–82) has discussed some of these issues at length and has shown convincingly that historical distance need not be an obstacle in the historian's understanding of the past, but rather has distinct advantages in that the lengthened perspective adds a deeper dimension to his historical understanding—a concept closely related to the workings of the enriched text. The telescoping of reception into one compound text does more than provide us with an example of multiple readings; it gives the contemporary reader insight in the direction in which the text moves, opening him to the future of the text and encouraging him to complete his own reception in new and different circumstances.

The Problem of Reference

The third and final methodological problem we shall be discussing here is the question of reference. Perhaps nowhere else does the difference between the historical and structural approach become so clear as in this issue. Ever since Gottlob Frege introduced the distinction between "Sinn" and "Bedeutung" (cf. Ricoeur, 1976:19; Thiselton 1980:122), the meaning of discourse has been fragmented into the *what* ("Sinn" or sense) and the *about what* ("Bedeutung" or reference) of the text. The structural approach, with its emphasis on the autonomy of the text, is primarily interested in the *internal* relations of the text—consciously excluding any considerations foreign to the text itself—thereby concentrating on the *sense*. The historical approach sees the text as a product of a genetic process, and is therefore mainly interested in the relationship between the text and the external factors surrounding its origin, thereby concentrating on the *referential* aspect.

We have already emphasized that the autonomy of the text is always of a relative nature. We should therefore take heed of Krieger's warning against any sterile contrast between texts viewed as windows, opening up on the preliterary history of their parts, and as mirrors on whose surfaces we find self-contained worlds (cf. Petersen 1978a:24). At stake here is the much wider issue of the relationship between text and "reality" which is too complex to be treated in terms of a simplified either/or choice. Reference is a multi-dimensional phenomenon and should be respected as such.[3] What we propose to do here is take a concrete example, namely Jesus' dialogue with the Pharisees according to Matthew 23, and try to establish the various levels of referential meaning important for the interpretation of the text. The choice of this chapter was motivated by the fact that we find here an interesting interplay between historical and structural aspects.

The text of Matthew 23 can, of course, be approached in various ways. A historical-critical analysis would especially be interested in the origin and development of the text—in the historical circumstances referred to in the text, in the way Matthew utilizes his sources in the light of parallel passages, in the history of the separate traditions, and in the final redaction of the text. Questions like the following would be considered: Is the picture painted of the Pharisees historically accurate? Does this polemic reflect a later stage in the development of the early church?, and so on. We are deliberately not following this line of enquiry, but take our point of departure from an analysis of the structure of the chapter itself. By doing so, we hope to find a new perspective on the problems of reference, including the

[3] Cf. the cryptic formulation of N. Goodman (1981:20): ". . . Jede Wirklichkeit (ist) vom passenden Text abhängig, und jeder passende Text ist von einer Wirklichkeit abhängig, die textabhängig ist."

historical aspects mentioned above.

We shall proceed to summarize, in a very brief form, some of the more important results drawn from a structural analysis of Matthew 23, without discussing the technique, which has been described elsewhere (Lategan, 1978b:341–60). The chapter forms a literary unit, comprised of Jesus' speech against the Pharisees and the teachers of the Law. The first gospel is well-known for the way in which word and deed supplement one another, for example, the way in which the teaching of Jesus (e.g., chapters 5–7, 10, 13, 23–25) is interspersed with narrative sections about his deeds (chapters 8–9, 11–12, 14–16, etc.). Chapter 23 fits into this pattern and exhibits a number of features common to the other "teaching" sections. These include thematic similarities, as will be indicated, and remind us from the start that Matthew 23 as microstructure can only be understood within the macrostructure of the first gospel as a whole. The chapter itself comprises four syntactically marked sections:

> vv 1–12 : The works of the Pharisees
> 13–32 : The seven woes
> 33–36 : Judgement on the Pharisees
> 37–39 : Jesus' love for Jerusalem

In the first section the addressees (the people and the disciples) are warned against the *exemplum* of the Pharisees and the teachers of the Law, with the injunction:

> Do as they say, but don't do as they do
> —because they say and don't do. (v 3)

This paradox in the works of the Pharisees forms the basic structure of the section. On the one hand, there are only words and no deeds; on the other, it is these (non-existent) deeds or works ($\H{\epsilon}\rho\gamma\alpha$, v 5) that are the focal point. They lack the *right* deeds, but excel in the wrong *erga*. These wrong *erga* are further qualified as being done for "appearances' sake" (v 5)—to be seen by *men* (not God). In the new community, there is no hierarchy (v 8) or paternalism (v 9), but a new brotherhood of humility and service (v 11). In view of what follows, it is important to note that the reference to the Pharisaic customs is linked to a description of the community of faith.

The second part (vv 13–32) consists of a series of seven woes, introduced by the formula: "Alas for you, teachers of the Law, hypocrites!" A shift of audience takes place and the Pharisees are addressed directly. The reference is to four Pharisaic practices: proselytizing, oaths, tithes, and ritual cleanliness. Again the inside/outside or visible/invisible contrast is used (vv 26–28) and the "for appearances' sake" of verse 5 reappears. The ambivalence in what meets the eye—$\phi\alpha\acute{\iota}\nu\epsilon\sigma\theta\epsilon$ $\tau o\hat{\iota}s$ $\dot{\alpha}\nu\theta\rho\acute{\omega}\pi o\iota s$ $\delta\acute{\iota}\kappa\alpha\iota o\iota$ (v 28)—is repeated in the irony of the leaders who are seen but don't see themselves (vv 16, 19, 24) and continues the visible/invisible theme of Matthew 11–12.

In v 29 a very important transition takes place. Up until now the references to the Pharisees may be understood merely as illustrative material to warn against hypocrisy in general. But in this last woe, which formally still belongs to the second section, the theme of the third is already anticipated. The attention to the graves of the prophets and the pious assertions that they would have had no part in the murder of these righteous men, reveal their real descent—they are the offspring of the murderers of the prophets. By this move, the Pharisees are given a place in history and are exhorted to continue the work of their forbears (v 32).

The genealogical terminology is continued in the opening statement of the third section (v 33), where the Pharisees are called "offspring of vipers" and a little later "this generation." These are exactly the words used in Matt 12:34 ($\gamma\epsilon\nu\nu\acute{\eta}\mu\alpha\tau\alpha$ $\dot{\epsilon}\chi\iota\delta\nu\hat{\omega}\nu$) and 12:41 ($\tau\hat{\eta}s$ $\gamma\epsilon\nu\epsilon\hat{\alpha}s$ $\tau\alpha\acute{\upsilon}\tau\eta s$) to describe the Pharisees. In fact, the phrase is intensified in 12:39 and 45 to "this *wicked* generation." By this linking of Matthew 23 to Matthew 11–12, the macrostructure of Matthew as a whole is brought into play and we are forced by the text itself to take this wider context into account when attempting to interpret Matthew 23. As has been shown elsewhere (Lategan, 1977:115–29), Matt 11–12 reveals an antithetical structure (so typical of the first gospel as a whole), in which the various binary oppositions are grouped successively along a positive negative axis in the following manner:

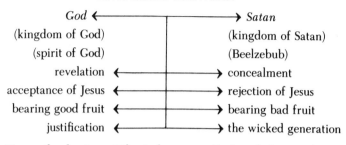

POSTITIVE   NEGATIVE

ANTITHESIS BETWEEN

God ←————————————————→ Satan

(kingdom of God)   (kingdom of Satan)

(spirit of God)   (Beelzebub)

revelation ←————————→ concealment

acceptance of Jesus ←————————→ rejection of Jesus

bearing good fruit ←————————→ bearing bad fruit

justification ←————————→ the wicked generation

From the basic antithesis between God and Satan, there is an inevitable progression down the line until the final division into two "families," two communities, two kingdoms, two modes of existence is completed. In Matthew 23 the Pharisees are clearly identified with the wicked generation, the murderers of the prophets, with the opponents of God himself during all of Israel's history. The chapter therefore is not a general and time-less warning against hypocrisy, using the Pharisees as illustration of a general human phenomenon, but is placed within a certain tradition, within the stream of history.

In v 37 at the beginning of the fourth section, a further shift takes place. The addressees are no longer the Pharisees, but Jerusalem itself. Although the second person plural reappears in vv 37c and 38, the scope is widened in v 37a. The Pharisees are super-seded by Jerusalem, the symbol of the Jewish nation as a whole. To Jerusalem are attributed the same works as to the Pharisees— killing the prophets and stoning the messengers of God (v 37). Therefore the announcement of judgement follows (v 38). Far from a moral lesson on hypocrisy, we see the first cracks that even-tually led to the split between church and synagogue.

From our analysis it becomes clear that the chapter forms a structured whole in which not only the accusations leveled against the Pharisees are presented in a stylized form but also the transi-tion from one section to the next is carefully marked. At the same time, thematic connections with the macrostructure give some indication of the chapter's relatedness to the "theology" of Mat-thew as a whole. Apparently, we are not dealing with a descriptive text, but with a narrative world (*erzählte Welt*) created by the text. The mode of reference therefore changes and we are fore-warned against the possibility of "referential fallacy," that is,

construing the signifier alone as the sign and as referring directly
to the real world, without regard to the signified as the conceptual
aspect of the sign (Petersen, 1978a:39). By this shift, the evidential
nature of the text is altered. Its primary function is no longer to
supply information about the social conditions or circumstances of
its origin but to serve as a vehicle of its "message." An illustration
of this change is the fact that Matthew 23 provides us with no
adequate answer to the question: Is the picture painted of the
Pharisees here historically accurate? Strack and Billerbeck (1926:
909–44; 1928:334–52; cf. also Finkel, 1964) provides us with rab-
binic parallels to prove the case, but these have been countered
with the argument that, although the description might fit the
worst of the Pharisees, it certainly is not true of the group as a
whole. Counter-examples are quoted to illustrate the humility and
self-denial of the Pharisees. Thus the historical issue remains
inconclusive. Haenchen (1951:38–62) realizes this problem and
differentiates between Jesus' own knowledge of the Pharisees and
the use Matthew makes of this conflict, giving recognition to the
role of the redactor in structuring the text. But then he explains
this shift in terms of a historical and sociological development:
Jesus himself was fully conversant with the varied nature of Pharisaic behavior, but at the time Matthew 23 was composed, the relationship between Jew and Christian had deteriorated so greatly
that appreciation of the more positive aspects of Pharisaic behavior was no longer possible.

It is ironic that the history of the subsequent interpretation of
Matthew 23 proved to be more a process of misreading than of
understanding the intention of the text. In most cases, the chapter
did not result in the communication suggested by our analysis.
Whereas the discourse initially refers to an antithesis *within* the
Jewish people, to two "genealogical" lines, two communities
within the parameters of its own tradition, this fine distinction
became blurred in the subsequent history of interpretation. The
Pharisees became identified with the Jews as such, resulting in the
rift between church and synagogue and determining to a large
extent the attitude towards, and treatment of, Jews by the church.
As a further twist of irony, the imagery of Matthew 23 was also
turned against the church itself. This happened when the plea for
the emergence of a "new community" was appropriated by radi-
cals who equated "Pharisees" not with the Jews but with the
church, as symbol of established and unflexible religious authority

representing vested interests (cf. Garland 1979:210–15; Schweizer 1973:291). This immediately raises the question of the role of the reader in assigning meaning to the text. Later generations of readers apparently were not merely passive receivers of Matthew 23 and its message, but actively reinterpreted it in a different setting, assigning more often than not "aberrant" readings to the text (Eco 1979:8). This chapter provides us with a concrete example of reader response—an issue which will be discussed in more detail in Chapter 3.

But let us, for the purpose of our present discussion, return to the various levels of reference. Let us take the shift in the mode of reference which we detected in Matthew 23 one step further. If, by the act of inscripturation (*Vertextung*) a certain measure of distance is achieved (from the author, from the situation of discourse, and from the original audience) (cf. Ricoeur, 1978b:229; cf. also Gadamer, 1975:3 on *Verfremdung*), it also implies that the text must no longer be seen as an *imitatio* of the real world. By slipping the painter from this one-to-one relationship with reality, the text is set free to sail under its own colors and becomes a creative force in opening up new possibilities for understanding and existence. The first order of reference is abolished in favor of a second order. An extreme but very striking example is Nathan's appearance before David after the death of Uriah (2 Sam 12; for a fuller interpretation of the story, cf. Chapter 3, p. 81, and Chapter 4 below). By beginning with a parable, the prophet deliberately draws David's attention away from his immediate personal situation. He then succeeds in bringing the king to a point where the latter identifies himself with the poor man and his one little ewe lamb. By doing so, Nathan is able to force David to accept a reality he has thus far chosen to ignore. The suspension of reality on the first level is a precondition for the *return* to reality on a different level. The text in this way becomes an illustration of Jüngel's thesis (1969) regarding the priority of possibility over against reality. By its refusal to accept reality as *the* final possibility, the text redescribes it in terms of a proposed world, opening up new possibilities for existence.

Does the change in the mode of reference and the *re-description* of reality[4] imply that the text is cut loose from its

---

[4] Both elements in the term "re-description" should receive equal weight to

historical moorings and that the exegete is no longer obliged to account for the historical aspects? We have already emphasized the *Geschichtlichkeit* of the text and of the communication process. We can now be more explicit about the various levels on which historical reference is essential for the successful mediation of the text.

On the most basic level, the reader must know what a phylactery is (Matt 23:5) or what deep fringes on robes signify in order to understand this verse. He must be conversant with the whole debate between the schools of Hillel and Shammai regarding ritual cleanness to make any sense of v 25.

Reference of the first order also functions on a second level, that of the reinterpretation of the text, by setting the outer limits of this operation. Matthew 23 is not intended to give us information regarding the social stratification of its original context, but the reference to the Pharisees does restrict the possibilities of *re*interpretation. The latter must be "true to type," or within the realm of the possible, in order to succeed as communication. Vorster (1980c:42–45; cf. also Du Plessis, 1980:25–41) quite correctly stresses the role of characterization as a literary device which first of all must be understood intertextually, but here again the limits of characterization are jointly set by precepts of common experience. The importance of the historical input on this level is even more fundamental; it is not restricted to random issues of historical interest, but, as Thiselton (1980:385) points out, the very grammar of the concepts involved is embedded in a history of events and behavior. "It is part of the grammar of the concept of 'God' that he is the God of Abraham, of Isaac, and of Jacob (Exod 3:6)."[5]

The final level of reference which will be considered here is that of the entire text as a communicative entity. We have seen how Matthew 23 is influenced on various strategic points by the wider plan of the gospel, and how themes from this chapter find their proper perspective against the background of the text as a whole. This *muthos* (Ricoeur's term: 1978b:244), this conceptual

---

stress both the continuity and discontinuity on the referential level.

[5] Ricoeur (1978a:197) maintains ". . . our ultimate interest when we do history is to enlarge our sphere of communication. This interest expresses the situation of the historian as belonging to the field that he studies. He is a member of his set of objects." For an even more fundamental view on the importance of biblical history, cf. Jüngel, 1978:296.

network of ideas, corresponds to what is usually called the "theology" of a biblical text. This framework not only gathers the various subthemes together—but also gives the final direction to the text. By doing so, the proposed world of the text comes into view, a world that the reader "might inhabit and project his own-most possibilities" (317). But this also represents the final phase of the interpretation process where the *Umweg* of the text via its structure and distancing nature leads the reader back again to rejoin "ordinary" reality—certainly not back to the point where he or the text started, but, as we have seen, the specificity of biblical language inevitably includes the historical dimension and places the reader before concrete options in the reality he finds himself. Matthew 23 spells out the two possibilities: either to continue the line of the "wicked generation" or to become part of that stream of history which represents the family of God. In the words of Gadamer (1975:274–75): *"Das Verstehen ist selber nicht so sehr als eine Handlung der Subjektivität zu denken, sondern als Einrücken in ein Überlieferungsgeschehen, in dem sich Vergangenheit und Gegenwart beständig vermittelt"* (cf. also Ricoeur, 1978a:198; Stuhlmacher, 1979:204). Our reflection on the important role historical reference plays in directing the reader to the future of the text leads us to agree with Jüngel's thesis: *"Das ontologisch Positive der Vergänglichkeit ist die Möglichkeit"* (1978:289). True historical interest is not aimed at establishing the pastness of the past, but at discovering its possibilities and finding the courage to realize them anew in the present.

2

Meaning and Reference:
The Parables of Jesus in Mark 4

Willem S. Vorster

It has become common practice to study the parables of Jesus in isolation from the contexts in which they were transmitted in the gospels. Since the days of Jülicher parable research has become synonomous with the study of the parables in the life of Jesus, that is, in their original form. This approach has been very fruitful and it undoubtedly contributed much to our understanding of the growth and transmission of the Jesus tradition. As a result of renewed interest and thorough research, especially in the United States, during the past decade much has been done to enrich our knowledge of the parable form, how it works, and what it refers to (cf. Harnisch, 1979, and Kissinger, 1979). Metaphoricity, narrativity, paradoxicality, and brevity have become common parlance with reference to the parables. The focus in these studies is still on the original form of these parables with a view to the historical Jesus (cf. Weder, 1978). There are many advantages, but since we are so taken up with the idea of reconstructing artifacts we do not always realize what the disadvantages of such an approach seem to be. One such a disadvantage is the fact that very often the written form of the parables is neglected because it is interpreted with a view to its original form and not within its later *written* context. The question of how parables mean, how they refer, and what they refer to are normally reserved for the parables of Jesus, that is, hypothetically reconstructed parables which only exist in our minds. I am of the opinion that the insertion of the parables into gospel narratives poses many a question which has not been appropriately investigated by New Testament scholars.

Jesus was a storyteller and so were many of the early Christians. The New Testament bears witness to this statement. First

of all, it contains a large number of stories of Jesus even though
they are in a retold form. In addition to that, a major part of the
New Testament consists of narrative literature. The parables of
Jesus are part of this narrative material and are themselves narratives. The parables of the gospels (embedded parables) are
retold stories. Because of their linguistic environment (context)
they should also be analyzed with a view to the purpose of their
retelling in a new environment.

Parables are a kind of narration: somebody tells *something*
to *somebody* about *something* which is worth telling (cf.
Polanyi, 1981b:98–99). It is within this process that parables
mean. Of interest for this chapter is how the *something* which is
told (narrative message) means and, furthermore the *about-what*
something is told, or: how does a parable refer? These questions
will, however, not be posed in connection with parables in isolation, that is, parables which are analyzed in isolation from the
context in which they occur in the gospels.

The problem I wish to consider is how do *embedded parables* mean, how do they refer, and what do they refer to? For
that purpose I have chosen Mark 4:1–34 which is presented to
the reader as a narrated "speech" of Jesus containing five (?)
parables and an interpretation of one of those parables. To put it
differently, the narrated Jesus is presented in a narrative framework as narrating narratives to somebody—that is, narrated narratives as talk (cf. Polanyi, 1981b). Let me first make a few
observations on meaning and reference.

In order to interpret the meaning of signs (words, symbols,
icons, parables, gospels, etc.) it appears to be of vital importance
to distinguish between meaning and reference. Meaning is
mainly a matter of relationships. These involve the relationship
between a sign and what it signifies (the *signified* or *signatum*),
signs and their relationship with signs in a series (for example,
words in a sentence), signs in contrast to other signs, and so on.
These relationships determine the meaning of signs, that is, how
they mean (cf. Nida, 1981; Fodor, 1977; and Scholes and
Kellogg, 1966:82). The meaning of a sign (its signified) should
not be confused with its referent. Reference has to do with the
thing (*denotatum*) to which a sign refers. A simple example
should suffice. The *meaning* of *ho ophis* ("snake") in Revelation
12:9 is "a kind of long, legless, crawling reptile," while its referent (*reference*) is the devil. This is basically the distinction

which Frege (1892) as a logician made between *Sinn* and *Bedeutung* (cf. Fodor, 1977:14; Ricoeur, 1975:81). In the words of Paul Ricoeur: ". . . meaning is *what* a statement says, reference is *that about which* it says it" (Ricoeur, 1975:81; cf. Nida, 1981:51). We shall return to Ricoeur's views on reference and the parables (p. 53). Suffice it to say that the implications of distinction between meaning and reference and the determining of the referent can be far-reaching for the interpretation of the parables, as is seen in the following example.

It is well-known that both Dodd and Jeremias, following Jülicher, used essentially the same historico-critical method in their attempts to determine what the parables meant in the time of Jesus. They were also in agreement that the parables had to be interpreted with a view to Jesus' eschatological preaching of the kingdom of God. They, however, interpreted eschatology, and for that matter the kingdom of God, differently. According to Dodd, Jesus' eschatological message was a *realized* eschatology while Jeremias regarded it as an eschatology in the process of being realized. It is clearly not a matter of difference of opinion about the meaning of "Kingdom of God" but about the *reference* of the term. For Dodd it referred to the rule of God which is at hand, present. For Jeremias it was different (cf. Dodd, 1936; Jeremias, 1970; and also Kümmel, 1982). That is why they arrived at two totally different interpretations of the parable in Mark 4:26–29. "In terms of this parable, therefore, we must conceive Jesus not as sowing the seed, nor yet as watching the growth and predicting a harvest in the future, but as standing in the presence of the ripe crop, and taking active steps to 'put in the sickle'" (Dodd, 1936:179). Unlike Dodd, who calls it the parable of the "seed growing secretly," Jeremias arranges the same parable under the heading of "the great assurance" ("Die grosse Zuversicht," cf. Jeremias, 1970:145) and calls it the "parable of the patient husbandman" ("geduldige Landmann," 151). According to him the parable gives the assurance that the time of harvest will come in the future. Everything must be left in the hand of God.

The implications of this example are clear. In cases where the referent of a sign has to be constructed it often leads to multiple interpretations. In view of this it has recently been argued that parables are plurisignificant, in other words, that each parable can have multiple meanings (cf. Wittig, 1977). One has to be clear about the difference between multiple meanings (polysemy) and multiple interpretations of the same sign. The latter speaks for itself. Anybody who has worked on the interpretation of a parable like that of the sower, for example, knows that the many interpretations given to the parable are the result of the way(s) in which the interpreter reads his text (cf. Brooks and Warren, 1970:336). In this sense, meaning is attributed to the text. That accounts for the multiple meanings (= multiple interpretations) which, as long as they can be validated, are normal and welcome. But are parables plurisignificant? Wittig argues that the parabolic sign (the parable as sign) "is a duplex connotative system in which precise significance is left unstated" (1977:84). According to her these signs have two referents. The one is directly supplied within the conventional code of the language, while the other has to be "supplied within the conventions of another sort of system: the system of beliefs and concepts held by the perceiver" (Wittig, 1977:85). It is in this second order that the reader creates or attributes a meaning to the text depending on his approach (be it historico-critical, Marxist, structuralist, or what have you). "The 'real meaning' of the parable, then, does not lie in the structure of the text, but in the *structuring* of the text—not in the created product but in the process of creation" (Wittig, 1977:95). The theory is not totally convincing. In the first place, multiple meanings and multiple interpretations are used as if they are the same thing. Furthermore, it seems that Wittig has misinterpreted the nature of the "second order referent," to stay within her model. The fact that the second order referent has to be constructed because it is out of our reach, since it "exists" only in the narrative world, does not mean that the sign is polysemic. We shall return to this problem below (p. 53) in our discussion of the parables and how they refer.

In order to determine whether a sign has different meanings or can be used for different meanings, there has to be a reasonable number of contexts available in which the *same* sign occurs. That we unfortunately do not have in the case of the parables. Thus we can only speculate about the possibility of a parable, or the parable and polysemy. From the history of parable research it is evident that many possible meanings or interpretations can be provided for one and the same parable, depending on the reader's approach.

Text type and context are also very important matters in describing meaning and reference. In characterizing the parables of Jesus, as I have mentioned, terms like metaphoricity, narrativity, paradoxicality, and so on serve as markers for the text type. According to Ricoeur (1975:88–89) parable has to be ". . . defined as the mode of discourse which applies to a *narrative form* a metaphoric process." This definition

> . . . conveys in a more technical language the spontaneous conviction of the lay reader that he has to do at the same time with a freely created story and with a transfer of meaning which does not affect this or that part of the story but the narrative as a whole, and which becomes in that way a fiction capable of redescribing life.

In other words, parables are extended metaphors and, as such, they mean and refer. To Wilder parables as metaphors are bearers of the reality to which they refer. "The hearer not only learns about that reality, he participates in it. . . . Jesus' speech had the character not of instruction and ideas but of compelling imagination, of spell, of mythical shock and transformation" (Wilder, 1971:84). And according to Funk (1966:134) they ". . . are open-ended," applicable to various situations with a ". . . potentiality for new meaning." Unlike Via (1970), who maintains that the parables are non-referential aesthetic objects which have meaning in themselves independent of their original setting, Ricoeur, like Crossan (1980:12), regards the referential aspect of the parables which he views as the redescription of reality (see below, p. 53) as very important. In addition he asserts that the plot, namely, ". . . the Kingdom is like what *happens* in the story" (1975:98), and the influence of the parables as "corpus" (1975:100ff.) are constitutive for the meaning of the parables. "Parables are stories given as fictions. But what they *mean* is . . . [that] the course of ordinary life is broken, the surprise bursts 'out'" (1975:103). In the bursting out of the surprise lies the extravagance (Ricoeur) and the paradoxicality (Crossan) of the parables. In this approach both the allegorical interpretation of the parables and the idea of Jülicher and his followers—that each parable has only one point to make—are rejected as possible means to describe the semantic aspect of parables.

It is in context that signs mean. This holds good for words, metaphors and parables. These signs are supposed to contribute to the context (cf. Brooks and Warren, 1970:458). Let us for a moment turn to the parable of the good Samaritan to illustrate what is involved. Stripped of its present context in the Gospel of Luke, this narrative presents a perfect example of the parable form even though it has traditionally been regarded as an example story. It is a complete short narrative with plot, characterization, point of view, implied author, and reader, and presents the reader "with a paradox involving a double reversal of expectations. The forces of good (Priest, Levite) do evil; the forces of evil (Samaritan) do good" (Crossan, 1976:260). In terms of the current debate on the parables, no doubt this story will be classified as a parable. It can be regarded as a metaphor on the kingdom of God. The metaphor is extended to a short narrative where the extraordinary becomes the ordinary (cf. Ricoeur, 1975:99). In view of its present context in the Gospel of Luke (10:25–36), however, where it has become part of a narrative on neighborly love, and especially because of the words "you go and do likewise" (v 37), it has traditionally been interpreted as an example of Christian conduct. In other words, how the parable means in Luke's Gospel is determined by its present context in that gospel. As a quoted narrative of Jesus within Luke's story about Jesus and the lawyer on neighborly love, it contributes to the meaning of the latter and also to the gospel as a complete narrative. "For a full elaboration of their meaning the parables are dependent on their context. Hence every different context into which they are placed will result in a different interpretation" (Tolbert, 1979:48). Like words, the meaning of parables seems to depend on the context within which they are used.

If we now turn our attention to Mark 4, the foregoing observations will inevitably lead us to investigate the problem of meaning and reference not only in terms of relationships between signs, signifieds, and referents, but also to aspects such as text type, context, and so on. The main focus is on how these embedded parables mean and refer in Mark 4.

Mark 4:1–34 and the Markan Narrative

Mark as narrative

It appears that there are only a limited number of ways in which discourse is organized, namely, narration, description, argument, dialogue, and lists (cf. Nida, 1981:29–30; Brooks and Warren, 1970:56–58). Obviously these forms can be mixed within the same text. Since meaning is organized differently in different kinds of discourse, it follows that any valid reading of a text will also depend on a correct understanding of the type of discourse involved. This goes for the gospels as well. There can be little doubt that the gospels are narratives. What this implies as regards the meaning of the gospels or parts of it is another matter. Important as other approaches like *Redaktionsgeschichte*, structural(ist) analysis, and others may be, it seems that they cannot offer an answer to the questions of how the embedded parables in Mark 4 mean and refer. This is a problem directly related to narrativity. I shall therefore elaborate on these problems in view of the aspects of narrative which constitute meaning, since the answer to these problems depends upon the fact that these parables form part of a narrative text. The decision of Mark to *write* a gospel was of major importance for the history of the Jesus tradition. The moment it was written down, Jesus, his words, and his works were presented in *one* specific way, from a specific angle. Even though that presentation is open to multiple interpretations, it still remains a single representation. This was only changed when a second and third and more gospels and other text types based on living oral tradition(s) came to be written (cf. Vorster, 1980c:36–38).

Closely related to the fact that these parables were embedded in a written text, and all that this implies, is the fact that they were embedded in a narrative text. Mark decided to organize the material which was transmitted to him into a narrative on aspects of the life and works of Jesus. He thus established perspectives through which the reader or hearer ". . . is presented with characters, actions, setting, and events which constitute the narrative . . ." (Abrams, 1971:133).

If we wish to determine how the meaning (the what) of a narrative text is constituted, we will have to analyze how the what (the narrative message) of the text as a narrative world functions. To put it another way, the narrative message of a text is constituted by space, time, plot, character, and point of view (cf. Vandermoere, 1976:1–7; Vorster, 1980a:126–30). Those are the aspects of interest for the answer to our problem of how these embedded parables mean, since they form part of a network of intersignification within this created narrative world, the story of Mark. Quite naturally our investigation of these matters will be limited to their relevance for Mark 4:1–34.

With the material transmitted to him through oral tradition, Mark created the space (from Galilee to Jerusalem), and the time (Isaiah, through the life and death of Jesus, to the coming of the Son of Man) of his narrative, plotted the events and actions and characterized the figures into a meaningful structure.

A few remarks on narrated time and space in the Markan story are necessary. The temporal coordinates of the gospel are set between the prophecy of Isaiah (1:2) and the coming of the kingdom with the return of the Son of Man (cf., e.g., 8:38). These are the time limits within which the narrative events take place. The movement (reading time) is not always the same. It takes much less time to read what happened between the above mentioned prophecy and the beginning of the Galilean ministry (1:1–15) than what happened during the few days in Jerusalem (11:1 and following chapters).

Time can be a very helpful technique in steering the reader's mind. This is the case with the previews and retrospection in the gospel. One of the best examples is the statement of the centurion at the cross, *alēthōs houtos ho ánthrōpos huios theou ēn*: "really this man *was* the Son of God" (15:39). Some of the previews are realized and others not. Although the death plot is introduced early in the narrative (3:6), it is interrupted by other more important themes which the author works out first. It is taken up again in 11:18 and worked out in the passion narrative. Reading Mark 4:1–34 as it stands, first of all, gives a very positive image of the disciples (cf. 4:10–12). But when the reader looks back at Mark 4 from the end of the gospel, the suggestions are there for a negative development in the story of the disciples (cf. Tannehill, 1977:398). The positioning of Mark 4 at that point of narrated time is very effective since hearing-and-understanding is an important motif in Mark's story (cf. the use of *akouō*, *suniēmi*, and related terms). Already at this stage it is suggested to the reader to listen carefully and identify with those who can understand.

Space is also used in narratives to make the story more effective. In the story of Mark, Galilee and Jerusalem are most probably not only geographical entities. They form part of the narrative world and its signification. This has been realized by Lohmeyer and has often been overemphasized by others (cf. Marxsen, 1959:33–76). In addition it is also very well-known that topological signs like "mountain," "sea," "house," "boat," and "on the road" have "special" meaning since they are used to create specific scenarios (cf. Vorster, 1980c:40). *Mountain* indicates the place where God is close and mysterious things happen (9:2); the *sea* is where the crowd receives teaching (cf. Chapter 4); whereas *house* is the place where Jesus acts and gives secret teaching to his disciples (cf. 7:17; 9:28; etc.). From 8:27 onward Jesus and his disciples are *on the road* (*en tē hodǭ*, cf. 8:27; 9:33; 10:32, 52; etc.). It is the passion road: from Galilee to Jerusalem. These spaces are used as signs which refer to spaces of closeness and distance between the characters involved. Mark used space, time, character, and plot very effectively in the transition from 3:31–35 to 4:1–34. We shall come back to this later.

"To follow a story, . . . is to understand the successive actions, thoughts, and feelings as having a *particular directedness*," says Ricoeur (1978a:182). This directedness of a story is effected, among other things, by the logical and causal arrangement of the narrated events, that is, by its plot. The plot of Mark falls into three parts, namely, 1:1–15 (beginning); 1:16–14:42 (middle) and 14:43–16:8 (ending). The middle (1:16–14:42) is a development of the themes given in the first part. Without going into detail, it will be necessary to draw attention to a few aspects of the plotting of Mark's story (cf. Vorster, 1980a:126–30).

The story Mark had to tell was about the significance of Jesus for the lives of his hearers (Tannehill, 1979:57). It presents Jesus the Son of God who has to suffer and die and who will return as Son of Man and what this implies for the reader/hearer. There are two narrative lines in his plot which are in constant tension and which are developed simultaneously, namely, the lines of victory and defeat. This is summarized by Barr: "It is correct, then, to see the action of Mark's Gospel as a movement from victory to defeat, from life to death, from openness to hiddenness. But within the defeat, the death, the hiddenness, Mark depicted the presence of God" (1977:105–6). From 1:16 through 8:27 the actions and events are plotted to present a gradual ascending line of victory for the protagonist. In 8:27 there is a turn in the story which reaches its low point in the death of Jesus but is suddenly reversed in 15:39 where the plot is resolved.

In the first half of the gospel Jesus is presented as the successful Son of God who conquers in everything he does or says. The events and actions are plotted in such a way that Jesus is always in a better position than any of the other characters. The reader is prepared for the other side of the coin by previews, narrative commentary, and so on (cf. 3:6; 3:19; etc.), but is nevertheless taken by surprise when Jesus rejects the confession of Peter in chapter 8 and spells out his suffering and death. The nonrealization of the expectations aroused by the plot leads the reader to critically revise his expectations of Jesus the Son of God as presented in the first half of the story. The programmatic unfolding of the second part of the gospel is structured by three sayings of Jesus (8:31; 9:31; and 10:33–34) foretelling the unfolding of the story.

It is well-known that the Markan Jesus is not as talkative as the Matthean or Lukan Jesus. He nevertheless delivers two major "speeches." The first is in Mark 4:1–34 and the second in Mark 13:5–37. One is given at the lake of Galilee and deals with the mystery of the kingdom of God, and the other on the Mount of Olives in which the coming of the Son of Man is of special interest. Both are part of the middle section of the plot of Mark's story which also contains other sayings. What Jesus has to say, when he says it, and how he says it form part of the way in which Mark organized his material into a meaningful structure.

After an initial announcement by Jesus that the time has come and that the kingdom is at hand (1:15), the story unfolds by presenting how it is at hand and why people should repent and believe the gospel. The events are plotted around the success of Jesus as the Son of God. He gathers helpers (1:16–20; 3:13–19) and teaches with authority (cf. 1:27); he heals (1:21–22 etc.) and is a master of words in controversies with Jewish leaders (cf. 1:5–12; 18–22). He forgives sins (2:1–11); changes Jewish practices (2:18; 2:23–128); and comes into conflict with his own family (3:31–134). Up to this point the central figure in the story, Jesus, is presented through characterization and plotting of the events as fulfilling his commission, namely, to show that he is the Son of God (cf. 1:9–11), in the face of opposition. The theme of opposition is carried to a climax in terms of plot, characterization, time and space in Jesus' quarrel with his family (3:31–34). In 3:23 he starts speaking *en parabolais* to the leaders opposing him. Now it is his relatives who are the opponents. His family is not his brother, sister, and mother, but those who do the will of God. What is remarkable about this micronarrative is, first of all, that Mark tells us that his family was standing *outside* (*eksō stēkontes*) and that he and *those around* him were in the *house* (cf. Kelber, 1974:26–27). In the next scene Jesus teaches the crowd at the *sea* in *parables*. After relating the parable of the sower he turns to the twelve and those around him. They are alone and he distinguishes between those *outside* (*tois eksō*), who receive everything *in parables*, and the *insiders*, the twelve and those around him. By putting these traditions into specific space and time settings in his narrative, Mark attempted to get his reader involved in the story of Jesus.

In structuring a narrative, characterization plays a very important role as we have already seen. It is also a vital aspect from the point of view of the reader/hearer. The way in which characters are presented directly influences the reader. No reader will identify with a character who is presented mainly in negative terms, whereas the opposite is true.

In the Gospel of Mark characterization takes place mainly through the narration of action. "We learn who Jesus is through what he says and does in the context of the action of others" (Tannehill, 1979:58). Jewish leaders including the scribes, Pharisees, and Sadducees are characterized negatively throughout the gospel. That is why the reader dislikes these characters and has sympathy with Jesus and what he says and does.

A very important group for our understanding of Mark 4:1–34 are the disciples. Perhaps they are to be regarded as the most complex characters in the gospel, also because they form part of the messianic secret. In the first part of the gospel there are three related scenes in which the disciples are given the function of "helpers" of Jesus in his own commission. These are the narrative of the call (1:16–20), the choosing (3:13–19), and the mission of the twelve (6:7–13). In these scenes the disciples are evaluated positively. In addition they are positively assessed in our chapter, namely in 4:10–12. Only once in the chapters preceding chapter 4 is there a negative remark about one of them (3:19). "Thus initial positive evaluation has an important function: it encourages the natural tendency of Christian readers to identify with Jesus' followers in the story" (Tannehill, 1979:71). By contrast with this positive presentation, there is a very strong negative characterization of the disciples. It starts with the pericope following our chapter (cf. 4:35–41). In three boat scenes where Jesus is alone with his disciples (4:35–41; 6:45–52; 8:14–21) they are presented as those who fear and do not understand. In 8:34–9:1 they are reestablished and commissioned to follow him even if it is difficult. Throughout the story, despite their close association with Jesus in everything he does and says, they fail to be his true helpers except for the open future and a promised meeting in 16:7. They are even replaced as helpers by other figures like Bartimaeus (10:52); the anointing woman (14:7–8); Simon of Cyrene (15:21); and the centurion at the cross (15:39). Tannehill, who has worked out extensively the characterization of the disciples in Mark, rightly remarks that the reader's initial expectations in connection with the disciples are not fulfilled. This leads to self-criticism and rethinking of what it means to follow Jesus. They nevertheless remain his followers and helpers until the end and this has a critical function for the reader. "When the disciples are in harmony with Jesus the author intends them to be viewed with approval; when they are not, with disapproval" (Tannehill, 1979:69).

"Those around" Jesus are also characterized positively as his followers. We have already referred to the very positive judgement of those around him in 3:31–5. In contrast to his family they are the people who do the will of God. They also appear on the scene in 4:10 where they and the twelve are those to whom the mystery of the kingdom is revealed. They see and understand.

Some of the recurring elements in the characterization of the crowds are: the fact that they are the ones who receive teaching (cf. 2:13; 4:2; 6:34; 8:34); their attraction to Jesus (2:4, 13; 3:22; 5:21, 24); their opposition to the religious leaders (11:18, 32; 12:12, 37); and Jesus' positive attitude towards them (cf. 8:2; 7:14). In chapter 14 there is an unexpected total break between them and Jesus and they join in the demand that Jesus be crucified (cf. 14:43; 15:8). "Stated in terms of personal relationships, the effect is similar to a close and trusted friend who has an opportunity to save a loved one and instead, for apparently political reasons, is instrumental in causing the loved one's death" (Boomershine, 1974:302).

The following characters from the main narrative, apart from Jesus, are involved in Mark 4:1–34: the crowd, those around him, the twelve (= the disciples), and those outside. How does the characterization of these narrated figures mentioned above affect the interpretation of Mark 4:1–34? As far as the crowd is concerned, one tends to appraise them positively as those who receive the teaching of Jesus and go wherever he goes. Verses 33 and 34, however, raise the question of whether they are not included with the outsiders to whom Jesus speaks in parables. The outsiders are characterized negatively as those who do not receive the mystery of the kingdom. They are continually looking but do not see, they listen but do not hear, and they will not repent and be forgiven (4:12). In view of the fact that the crowd eventually deserts Jesus and participates actively in his trial and death, it could be that they are already regarded as part of the outsiders in chapter 4. If so, the fact that they accompany Jesus from the beginning to the end, see, listen, are taught, and ought to know what he stands for, is all the more remarkable. They are then part of "those outside" who do not do the "will of God"—those who reject him.

The people around him and the twelve are those who are given the mystery of the kingdom. But they are also those who need special instruction. They ought to understand, but v 13 gives the impression that they do not seem to understand fully. This is only the start of the disciples' incomprehension, which is fully developed in the remainder of the story (cf. 4:41; 6:52; 7:18; 8:14–21; 9:10; 10:24, 26; and 14:40).

Mark 4:1–34 is a crucial point in the narrative as far as characterization is concerned. Up to this stage the reader is encouraged to identify with the disciples and the crowd, associate with them, and dislike the opponents. In a very subtle way the suggestion is made that the reader should think twice. Mark 4:11–12 is turned upside down in 8:17–18. The disciples do not understand! They have eyes but they do not see, have ears but cannot hear, and they do not understand. From now on there is a constant shift in identification between reader and narrated figures, fluctuating between sympathy, dislike, and pity. In 4:1–34 the reader is given a norm to evaluate the characters in the story and himself.

From the perspective of point of view there remain a few observations which will add to our understanding of how Mark 4:1–34 functions as part of the narrative and how the parables in that chapter mean.

We have noted above that Mark created perspectives from which the reader or hearer is presented with the characters and so on. This is what point of view is about. Mark made use of an omniscient and intrusive point of view, as I have suggested elsewhere (cf. Vorster, 1980b:58–61). The *narrator* of Mark's story knows everything about his characters: what they see, hear, feel, and even what they think (cf. 3:6; 5:28, 33; 6:49; 11:31; 15:10).

He knows the mind of Jesus (cf. 2:8; 3:5; 5:30). By arranging his material to suit his purpose, the focus is on the opposition Jesus experienced from the Jewish leaders. They are not only narrated; they are evaluated. For the sake of the reader he comments on strange words and phrases (cf. 3:17; 5:9; 5:41; 7:2, 11, 34; 10:46), uses *gar* in narrative commentary to explain (cf. 1:16, 22, 38), and lets his characters speak in the way he prefers.

What is the function of Jesus' "speech" in Mark 4:1–34 with reference to point of view? From chapter 1 to the end of chapter 3 Jesus is not very talkative, but what he says is of the utmost importance both for the way in which he is characterized (cf. 1:25, 35; 2:8, 17) and for our understanding of how the narrative means (1:15; 1:44; 2:5).

From what he says the reader knows his purpose and what he stands for. Like the narrator of the story he is omniscient. He even knows the thoughts of men and tells them that he knows what they think (2:8). From what he says the reader can gather who he is. He is an authoritative leader of people (cf. 1:17; 2:14, 17); he is a miracle worker (1:41; 2:5, 11, 23; 3:3, 5) who commands demons (1:35); he lays down new norms for forgiveness (2:5), fasting (2:18), the sabbath (2:23), and blasphemy (3:23–29); he is a teacher (cf. 3:23–29). He is the type of character with whom the reader would identify. However, the most important thing is that:

> Jesus's voice provides an evaluative context for understanding the speech and action of the crowds, because Jesus teaches them in a form designed to keep them ignorant of the kingdom, and for understanding the speech and actions of the disciples, because Jesus says that they, like the crowds, are without understanding. And it is Jesus's speech that provides an evaluative context for understanding the words and deeds of the authorities, because it is his speech that corrects and condemns them. (Petersen, 1978b:109).

From the perspective of point of view it should be noted that three of the public "speeches" of Jesus in the Gospel of Mark are said to have been *en parabolais*, namely, 3:23–29 on Beelzebul; 4:2–32 (the parable speech); and 12:1 on the parable of the vineyard and the tenants. These must be related to Mark 4:11–12 and 34, where he explicitly states that Jesus made a distinction in his teaching between the twelve and those around him on the one hand, and the outsiders on the other. The distinction between *en parabolais* and the possession of the *mystērion tēs basileias* is very important. The translation "in parables" fails to render the specific Markan distinction between overt and secret or mystery and riddle. "Figurative meaning" is perhaps the most distinctive feature of *en parabolais*, although not necessarily in a technical sense. In that sense the sayings regarding the lamp (4:21) and the measure (4:24) are also parabolic, that is, "parables." Kelber correctly observes:

> . . . everything is or *occurs in riddles* to the outsiders (*ta panta ginetai*). This is neither a statement on Jesus' specific use of parables, nor even on the purpose of his teaching in general, but on the nature of his ministry as a whole. The whole ministry is *en parabolais*, i.e. an enigma to outside recognition. This points beyond a specific theory on parables! (1974:32–33)

"Talking in parables," in other words, forms part of the way in which the narrated Jesus of Mark speaks to the outsiders, and is directly related to Mark's dialectic of hearing and understanding the message of the kingdom. The purpose is to encourage the reader to get involved in the message of the story of Jesus. Point of view is one of the techniques narrators use to get their story across. It is within this context that the function of the quotation of Isaiah 6:9 in Mark 4:12 has to be viewed.

Mark 4:12 is a well-known *crux interpretum*. It is normally regarded as Mark's view on the purpose of the parables. It has given rise to many theories on the rejection and punishment of Israel. "Als solche dienen sie (sc. die Gleichnisse) dem Zweck, die Wahrheit zu verhüllen, um über das widerspenstige Volk das Verstockungsgericht zu verhängen" (Gnilka, 1979:170).

In view of the function of Old Testament quotations in Mark, this seems to me rather doubtful. The quotation should be interpreted as part of the narrative point of view of the gospel and in the light of the motif of *understanding* why Jesus the Son of God had to suffer. Petersen rightly reminds us ". . . that the speech of all characters, including Jesus, is ultimately controlled by the external point of view of the narrator. His plotting of their speeches is an expression of his own ideological standpoint" (Petersen, 1978b:109), that is, his own conceptual understanding of the world he narrates.

I have elsewhere commented on the function of the use of

the Old Testament in Mark and need not repeat everything.
Most important is the fact that quotations from the Old Testament have the same function in Mark as narrative commentary
(cf. Vorster, 1981a:62–72). It *substantiates* the train of thought.
The quotations are often so well integrated into the narrative
that they form part of the narrative statement (cf. 1:1–4; 7:6–8;
10:5–8 and 14:27–28). It is often only because of the way it is
printed in our modern editions of the New Testament that we
read them as quotations. More often they sound like the words
of the narrator or narrated figures. It is remarkable that most of
the quotations from the Old Testament in Mark are in the
mouth of Jesus. They form part of the characterization of Jesus
and his opponents (cf. 7:6–7). The theme of incomprehension of
the disciples, referred to above, is brought into focus in Mark
4:12 (cf. 8:18) when Jesus uses the words of Isaiah 6:9–10, and so
also the whole matter of *understanding* why Jesus, the Son of
God, had to suffer. Because of the network of signification in a
text it would be wrong simply to read Mark 4:12 as an isolated
quotation on the parables and their meaning. Mark is not
explaining the purpose of the parables in the sense of a "Ver-
stockungstheorie." Kelber reminds us that the parable of the
sower is not introduced as *a* parable but as teaching *en parabolais* (plural).

> To the outsiders Jesus relates in parabolic riddling fash-
> ion, but the insiders will be given a chance to learn that
> he was actually lecturing on the present state of the
> Kingdom. Rather than punish, the parables will help to
> reveal what to the outside forms an inaccessible riddle,
> and to the inside takes on the appearance of a mystery.
> Basically, what the Galilean speech advances is a further
> elaboration of the Kingdom theme, but not a thesis on
> parables. (1974:33)

Mark 4:10–12 depicts Jesus in relation to his associates and to
those outside. This relationship is a complex one. It has already
been referred to in the preceding part of the narrative (3:31–35)
and is developed at length in the rest of the gospel. In fact, it
starts in the next verse (4:13). The reader is urged to look, listen,
and understand, and notice how insider and outsider alike fail to
understand the mystery of the kingdom of God.

Narrative commentary, which is a form of narrative point of
view, also directs the reader. In his attempt to help his reader/

hearer Mark often uses *gar* to indicate how the reader should understand some point or other (cf. 1:16, 22, 38; 2:15; 3:10). There are two important instances of *gar* in Mark 4:1–34.

It has often been a point of discussion whether or not the Q-logia in Mark 4:21–25 should also be regarded as "parabolic" or "parables." It seems to me that the use of *gar* in vv 22 and 25 can help us. The word indicates how the reader should regard the preceding sayings. Verses 22 and 25 are to be regarded as commentary on the logia preceding them, in the same way as 14–20 should be regarded as commentary on 3–9. Verses 22 and 25 are explanations of vv 21 and 24.

In Mark 4:1–34, as elsewhere in the gospel when Jesus speaks, the focus is not on why he says so little but on what he says and why he says it. As with all the other saying of Jesus in Mark, the function of the speech is first of all to create an evaluative context for the reader. Besides the information it offers on how things happen in the kingdom of God, it also provides the reader with norms to evaluate the actions of other characters in the story. These include the disciples, those outside, the crowd, and others who participate in the development of the story of Jesus, the Son of God who has to suffer and die in order to fulfill his commission.

How Do the Parables in Mark 4:1–34 Mean?

In order to determine how the parables in Mark 4 mean, it is necessary not only to see chapter 4 of Mark's Gospel as part of the Markan narrative world (as we have done above), but also to examine how the speech is organized internally. Broadly, the speech is structured as follows (cf. also Lambrecht, 1969:106ff., especially 109):

> Introduction (1–2): Setting (Jesus by the sea of Galilee teaching the *ochlos*)
>
> *kai elegen autois . . .*
> Akouéte (3)
> Sower (3–8)
> *kai elegen, Hos échei ōta akouein akouetō* (9)
>
> Once they were alone, those around him and the twelve enquired about the parables.
> (Change of setting) (10)

kai elegen autois (11)

> The mystery of the kingdom of God is explained
> to those inside. To those outside everything
> comes in parables (+ Isaiah 6:9) (11–12).

kai legei autois (13)

> Because they do not understand he gives an
> explanation of the parable to those who are sup-
> posed to understand (14–20).

kai elegen autois (21)

> "Parable" of lamp (21)
> Explanation of (*gar*) (22)
> *ei tis echei ōta akouein akouetō* (23)

kai elegen autois, Blepete ti akouete (24)

> "Parable" of measure (24)
> Explanation (*gar*) (25)

kai elegen (26)

> *houtōs estin hē basileia tou theou hōs* . . .
> Self-Growing Seed (26–29)

kai elegen

> *Pōs homoiōsōmen tēn basileian tou theou, ē en
> tini autēn parabolę thōmen; hōs* . . .
> Mustard seed (31–32)

Conclusion (33–34)

> Jesus preached his message to the people (*autois*), using
> many other parables like these; he told them as much as
> they could understand (*kathos edynanto akouein*). He
> would not speak to them without using parables, but
> when he was alone with his disciples, he would explain
> everything to them. (*TEV*)

The "speech" forms a self-contained unit with a beginning
and an end, although it has often been pointed out that it must
have grown in the transmission of the tradition (cf. Kuhn,
1971:99; Weder, 1978:99). For our purpose we are interested not
in the growth of the text but in its final form. Whether it is a
coherent text or not is significant only inasmuch as this affects
our interpretation. Since we have dealt with the characters of
the main narrative involved in the speech we need not repeat
this.

The discourse consists of a narrative framework (1–2 and

33–34) interspersed with seven quotations. Each quotation has a narrative introduction (cf. *kai elegen ktl.* in 11, 13, 21, etc.). Because of the theme of the kingdom of God, which plays a role from vv 3 to 32, it is regarded as a discourse and not as separate units of unrelated speech (cf. Delorme, 1979:157–91).

As for the coherence of the discourse, the audience remains a problem. The narrative starts with Jesus and the *ochlos* (and the twelve *cum suis?*). In v 10 there is a change of setting. The disciples and those around him are alone with Jesus. There is no indication in the remainder of the speech that the insiders have returned to join the crowd. This causes a problem. It is impossible to determine with certainty whether *autois* in vv 21 and 24 includes the crowd and the insiders, or whether the term refers to the insiders only. In 26 and 30 the audience is not mentioned at all, while the crowd (outsiders) seems to form part of the *autois* of v 33. That is why scholars have often drawn attention to the (so-called) tension between vv 33 and 34. These verses should, however, be regarded as a general summary. The *TEV* translation above renders the Greek well. The tension between 33 and 34 strikes one as more or less serious, depending on how one interprets the *autois* in vv 21 and 24 and the intended audience of vv 26 and 30.

The expression *kai elegen* in vv 26 and 30 is striking. It is used only in this instance and in v 9 in the speech. Verse 9 seems to round off the parable of the sower. If the phrase has the same function in vv 9, 26, and 30, it would imply that from 10 to 33 Jesus was addressing the insiders only.

One could also argue, however, that except for vv 10–20 or 10–25 the entire speech is addressed to the crowd.

The complete discourse is built around v 11, in which the *hiddenness* and *revelation* of the kingdom of God are the central focus. All five "parables" to some extent illustrate the hiddenness and revelation of the kingdom of God. First there is the *logos* motif, which occurs nine times in the speech. It has the meaning of "message" and refers to the preaching of the gospel (of the kingdom of God). The teaching of Jesus (v 3) is therefore aptly summarized in v 33 as *elalei autois ton logon*. It is this teaching, his message of the kingdom of God, which is both hidden and revealed.

The recurring motif of *akouō* is also prominent. The word occurs no fewer than thirteen times in the thirty-four verses.

Apart from its prominent use in the Old Testament quotation in
v 12, it is used in formulas which appeal to the reader, urging
him to listen attentively and become one of the insiders (9, 23,
24, cf. 33). In the interpretation of the parable of the sower
(14–20), the focus is on *hearing* the word.

It is in this context that we have to pursue the question of
how the parables of Mark 4 mean.

Elsewhere (cf. Vorster, 1981b) I have drawn attention to the
fact that the meaning of the parable of the sower in Mark's
gospel is obscured by the modern search for the "original meaning" of the parables as spoken by Jesus (cf. Crossan, 1980:25;
Carlston, 1975:137). In this search the *relationship* in Mark's
narrative between the parable of the sower in 4:3–8 and its
interpretation in 4:14–20 is neglected. The two "texts" are normally analyzed in isolation, and each is assigned its own meaning. It is usually argued that Mark 4:3–8 presents us with an
earlier form of the parable than the exposition given in 4:14–20.
The latter, it is argued, originated from the primitive church
and, since it gives an allegorical (metaphorical, according to
Weder, 1978:112) interpretation of parts of the parable, it should
be treated as secondary. Without submitting any reasons Gnilka
(1979:161) in his recent commentary on Mark offers an explanation of the meaning of the parable and then asserts that Mark
did not care for this particular meaning. According to him,
Mark accepted the "allegorical interpretation" in 4:14–20 as the
meaning of the parable. To avoid the problem of whether Jesus
could have used allegory or allegorical interpretation, which has
been denied since the days of Jülicher, Pesch calls it "eine
allegorisierende Parabel" (1976:229). Schmithals, on the other
hand, maintains that both the text (4:3–8) and its interpretation
(14–20) are the work of the narrator who was responsible for the
Grundschrift Mark used in writing his gospel. Accordingly, the
parable has one meaning only, and that is the "allegorical interpretation" in Mark 4:14–20. Mark accepted this meaning (cf.
Schmithals, 1979:231–33).

This inevitably leads to the conclusion that Mark's text and
what he says are not taken seriously. In answering the question
of how the parables in Mark 4 mean, it is beside the point
whether the parable of the sower as spoken by Jesus originally
had another meaning than the one put into his mouth in Mark
4:14–20. Mark edited and contextualized its interpretation for a

specific purpose. By inserting vv 11–13 between the parable and its interpretation, Mark told his story from his own perspective. The very fact that he tells the story of Jesus in this particular way forms part of the composition of the narrative. It is highly significant that he has Jesus, the teacher, tell a story and also explain it to the disciples who are presented as those who, despite their special instruction, often misunderstand Jesus. The only meaning the parable of the sower has in the Markan gospel is that given in the explanation of 4:14–20. This has consequences for our question of how these parables mean. We here have a very rare phenomenon in that the author of the text tells the reader explicitly how to understand a part of his text. The reader should note that the meaning of the parable is explained in relation to the word (*logos*). The sower sows the word. *Logos*, as we have noted, refers to Jesus' message of the kingdom. Each scene of the original story is interpreted in terms of how, under varying conditions which influence their reception, people *hear the word* (compare vv 3 and 14; 4 and 15; 5–6 and 16–17; 7 and 18–19; and 8 and 20). Since the parable is a short story marked by characterization, plot, and so on, it is remarkable that both the order of the scenes of the parable and the plotted line are retained in the exposition. Not every aspect of the original story is assigned a meaning—only those which relate to "hear," "the seed," and the conditions which permit or preclude fruitfulness.

Kelber (1974:27) correctly observes that the *logos* is the main protagonist, who suffers several defeats and gains a resounding victory: "A threefold failure is set over against a threefold success, but it is the period of crisis to which special importance is attached." This is the mystery of the kingdom revealed: continuous failure, but eventual success. In our attempt to answer how the parable means, two things should be kept in mind. Firstly, it is in keeping with the motifs of "hearing" and the "word," and also with hiddenness or the figurative meaning of the parable of the sower, that parts of the story are explained in *context* in a metaphorical (allegorical?) way: the seed is the word, and so on. But secondly, it is important to note that the *story* character of the original parable is retained. It is plotted in accordance with the plot of the first story. That is why one may well ask whether Mark 4:14–20 is not a *retelling* of the same story as the one in 4:3–8.

From a literary point of view, but also in view of the relationship between the written and oral forms of the stories of Jesus, the question is: should one not consider seriously the problem of whether the same story can be told twice (cf. Polanyi, 1981a)? This is a fine example of the problem attending the parables of Jesus. How the story of the parable of the sower means in Mark 4 is directly dependent on the fact that its reinterpretation is a *story that is retold*. The parable of the sower in Mark 4:14–20 is based on the same matrix as mark 4:4–8 (cf. Polanyi, 1981a:332). The same narrative time, space, and plot are found in both stories. The characters—the protagonist as well as the opponents—are different. By filling out the metaphorical characters, Jesus is presented as having told the same story twice, that is, a new story under new circumstances (contra Huffman, 1978:212). It is the same plot which brings about the same paradox. In relating the ordinary, the extraordinary is told by plotting the events into a hyperbole of a threefold "failure" and a threefold "success." Through the unusual "syntactic" (metaphor) and semiotactic arrangement of the plot the story has its impact.

It is noteworthy that Mark 4:3–8 is written as *narrative discourse (erzählte Welt)*, whereas the explanation in 4:14–20 is *direct discourse (besprochene Welt)*. In other words, the parable itself is recorded in narrated form and its explanation is a discussion of the parable in narrated form. Put another way, the parable of the sower in Mark 4 is presented as narrative within a narrative, whereas its explanation is a narrated discussion within the narrative. Both are, however, *narratives*. In terms of the structure of Mark's narrative, in which narrative discourse and direct discourse are continually alternated, and where the sayings of Jesus, as we have seen, often serve the function of presenting the reader with norms, this is not without significance. It gives an indication of how the author wished his readers/hearers to interpret the retold story. It tells us how the parable of the sower *means* in the Markan gospel. What this story means is explained first of all by how it means. In the retelling of the story the metaphorical process is extended in narrative form by filling out the characters by means of motifs, such as "word," which are important for the main narrative. The retold story, as well as the original version, refer to the kingdom of God in the Markan narrative—that is, as *Mark* presented the kingdom.

According to Mark, things happen in the kingdom as they happen in the retold story of the sower. This illustrates some of the consequences of reading the parables in their gospel contexts and also of reading them as (metaphorical) narratives.

It was said above that the sayings about the lamp and the measure are to be seen as parables or parabolic sayings which, on the strength of the use of *gar* in Mark, should in each case be explained in terms of the meaning supplied in the saying following it. This is how the author leads his hearers to understand Jesus' teaching on the kingdom. Although it is a mystery it will of necessity be revealed like a lamp, which is made to reveal light. But it should also caution the hearer/reader to be on the alert (cf. pp. 74–75) because in the measure that he accepts the kingdom he will be measured. The figurative meaning of these sayings is what counts. That is because he who has (insight into the kingdom of God) will be given more, and he who has nothing will forfeit even what he has. This is the way of the kingdom.

How is this message (meaning) created in Mark? Once again the context of the Markan narrative has to be kept in mind, and especially the context of Mark 4:1–34. The parable of the lamp is explained in terms of what is hidden and what is revealed. It is reiterated in the form of a chiasm:

a   *b*

ou gar estin krypton ean mē hina phanerothę̄,

b'   *a'*

oude egeneto apokruphon all' hina elthę̄ eis phaneron

The parable of the lamp is a metaphor of the kingdom of God in which the reversal of the order of hidden and revealed is underlined. It has a strong eschatological tone, strengthened by *hina*. Nothing is hidden unless it is in order that (so that) it will be revealed. The hidden kingdom will be revealed. Again the reader is urged to listen carefully (v 23). The same basic technique of creating meaning is used in the parable of the measure. An explanation is given in v 25. "Those who acknowledge and live according to the conditions set by the invisible Kingdom, will be rewarded, and they will be rewarded beyond all expectations" (Kelber, 1974:39).

How these parables mean is not very different from how the parable of the sower means in Mark. The same technique is applied. The metaphorical statements about the lamp and the measure are explained through a reformulation. The point of these reformulations is made in the context. Removed from this context, these sayings would have totally different meanings (cf. Luke 8:16–18). There is little doubt that ultimately the context of these sayings is the only factor determining what they mean. In the case of the parable of the sower, meaning was created by retelling the story in accordance with its new context. The two parabolic sayings about the lamp and the measure were reformulated in the sayings following each one to refer to a certain aspect of the kingdom.

As to the parables about the seed growing secretly and the mustard seed; except for contextual indicators we have no direct clues from the text how the author meant the reader/hearer to understand them. It is nevertheless clear that these parables' meaning refers to the kingdom, as their introductions indicate.

The parable of the growing seed (4:26–29) is introduced by the formula "the kingdom of God is like. . . ." In the end it is only a technicality whether one regards it as metaphor or comparison. It is the unusual syntactic and semiotactic arrangement of the "kingdom," and the story which affects the meaning. In other words, what matters is the predication of the kingdom of God by an extended narrative. The kingdom "is similar to that which *happens* in" the story of the seed growing secretly (cf. Ricoeur, 1975:98). The narrative is structured as follows:

a   b

⌐*anthrōpos balē ton sporon epi tēs gēs*
| *kai katheudē*
⌐*kai egeirētai nykta kai hēmeran,*

a'

⌐*kai ho sporos blastą*
⌐*kai mēkynētai*
⌐*hōs ouk oiden autos.*

b'

⌐*automatē he gē karpophorei, prōton chorton, eita*
| *stachyn, eita plērēs sitos en tǭ starchï.*
⌐*hotan de paradoi ho karpos, euthys apostellei to*
    drepanon, hoti parestēken ho therismos.

The narrative is structured by its plot, characterization, and by narrative commentary. The repetition of seed (a, a') and earth (b, b') draws attention to these components. The seed, the protagonist of the story, yields a harvest, with the aid of the "earth" which acts as "helper." Seed and earth seem to be the characters which are developed in the story, and not the man, since he only features in the opening scene where he introduces the construction of the plot. The story is told in time sequence from sowing to harvest. The whole story is told in direct discourse (*besprochene Welt*) and not in narrative discourse (*erzählte Welt*), which strengthens both its evaluative and its informative function. In the main story we are told that Jesus narrated the story. In his description (direct discourse) he characterizes the narrated figures. The sower sows and then comes and goes only to wait for the harvest. As far as the growing of the seed is concerned he is not active (cf. Carlston, 1975:204). The seed grows in a surprising way as the narrative commentary indicates (*hōs ouk oiden autos*). This is highlighted by the automatic (*automatē*) way in which the earth yields fruit; stage after stage follows until the crop is ready to be harvested. This idea is established by an allusion to Joel 3(4):13. It drives home the idea that the harvest is assured. "From sowing to harvest is a sure and certain step" (Carlston, 1975:205). The plot is again worked out in the form of a hyperbole, affecting a contrast between beginning and end. The emphasis is on the surprising automatic movement from the beginning to the final stage.

The Markan context suggests that both "kingdom of God" and "word" are important clues to the meaning and reference of the parable. The way in which the *logos* grows is hidden and astonishing. The harvest is guaranteed because the *logos* will bear fruit, thus affirming the mysterious workings of the kingdom. The evaluation of the characters in terms of surprise and certainty has the function of encouraging those who are able to hear.

How the story means is determined by its context and text type. It is a metaphoric narrative within a narrative context. In that context the referents are filled out.

The last in the series, namely the parable of the mustard seed, is the third seed parable in the speech. It is again introduced by a formula inquiring into the nature of the kingdom: "With what can we compare the kingdom of God? or what parable shall we use for it?" The second part is simply a repetition of the first. The kingdom is compared to. . . . Things happen in the

kingdom as in the story of the mustard seed. The plot is structured in two scenes:

> *hōs kokkǭ sinapeōs*
> *hos hotan sparę̄ epi tēs gēs mikroteron on pántōn tōn*
> *spermátōn tōn epi tēs gēs,*
> *kai hotan sparę̄, anabainei*
> *kai ginetai meidzon pantōn tōn lachanōn*
> *kai poiei kladous megalous, hōste dynasthai hypo tēn*
> *skian autou ta peteina tou ouranou kataskēnoun.*

The parable of the mustard seed, like that of the seed growing secretly, is narrated in direct discourse (*besprochene Welt*),
reinforcing the evaluative and informative function in the main
discourse. In Luke 13:18–19 it is rendered in narrated discourse
(*erzählte Welt*). Contrast between small and large is emphasized
by the focus on *mikroteron* and *meidzon*. There is one character, the mustard seed, and there are two plotted scenes. The
beginning is small, the ending great. The allusion to Daniel 4 in
v 32 is a qualification of the greater ending, which probably
refers to the fact that the kingdom "provides protection for all
who seek its shelter" (Carlston, 1975:159). The story is plotted
hyperbolically.

Meaning is established through contrast and characterization
in a narrative form. In the Markan context, seed most probably
refers to the message of the kingdom. In the kingdom things
happen to that message, just as things happen in the story of the
mustard seed. Carlston (1975:159) correctly remarks: "Mark's
tradition, however, probably did not stress the contrast . . . the
parable was probably still understood primarily in terms of the
symbol of birds and branches, as a reference to the inclusion of
Gentiles in the growing church as in Q."

If we return now to the speech as a whole, and as part of the
Markan narrative, there are quite a number of indications of
how the parables and parabolic logia of Jesus in Mark 4 should
be read, or how they mean. First of all, we have a clue in the
way the speech is structured. It is presented as part of a narrative. What Jesus says within this narrative is quoted in the form
of sayings and narratives. Unlike the parable of the sower, all
the other sayings and parables are given in direct discourse
(*besprochene Welt*), emphasizing their value as normative statements regarding the kingdom. The reader is involved in a complex narrative context, characterized by a deepening interest in

the distinction between the opponents and helpers of the protag-onist. Secondly, the narrative shows the insiders as the only ones able to understand Jesus' parables, but since they did not under-stand the parable of the sower, the narrative tells how they are enabled to understand the parables. How is this done? In the case of the parable of the sower, meaning is created by retelling the story in narrative form in a narrative context. The parabolic sayings are reformulated in accordance with the context. The other two parables, which are not expounded, are to be read as stories quoted in context. Narrativity remains their basic charac-teristic. By plotting the events in the form of hyperboles or para-doxes in all three cases, the extraordinary quality of the kingdom is rendered in terms of the ordinary (cf. Ricoeur, 1975:99). That is what the reader has to note and pursue.

Reality Remade, or How Do These Parables Refer?

In the introduction above I referred to the opinion of Ricoeur who, in opposition to modern literary criticism, maintains that poetic language such as that of the parables does have a referential function since "discourse is open and turned toward a world which it wishes to express and to convey in language" (Ricoeur, 1975:82). He believes that language is a closed system and that the above-mentioned use of reference is applicable only to signs within a language and not to signs within a text like a narrative. But in view of the fact that discourse is based on "a unit of genre, completely different from the units of language which are signs" (Ricoeur, 1975:81), namely, the *sentence*, its referential aspect is totally different. He argues that the characteristics of a sentence are in no sense a repetition of those of language. That is why a sentence's characteristics of meaning and reference are totally different from those of language signs. In view of this hypothesis, and such theo-ries as Max Black's theory of models, he introduced Mary Hesse's concept of redescription in connection with the referential aspect of the metaphor. In the case of the metaphor, the first order refer-ence (literal interpretation) is lost (cf. Wittig, p. 30 above), result-ing in a reinterpretation of reality which brings forth a second order reference, namely, a redescription of reality as a possibility of "the forming of the world" (cf. Ricoeur, 1975:82). Reference as redescription is "the movement of the internal structure of the work toward its reference, toward the sort of world which the

work opens *in front of* the text" (Ricoeur, 1975:82). This is very
important since, for Ricoeur, reference of a second order is quite
unlike reference of the first order. The latter is a movement *backwards* from the sign to what it refers to in the extralinguistic world,
whereas second order reference points forward (to an open possibility). "This hypothesis marks our complete break with structuralism where language functions purely internally or immanently,
where an element refers only to another element of the same system" (Ricoeur, 1975:81).

Although Ricoeur has been criticized for this view (cf. Crossan, 1980:12) it was welcomed by others (cf. the preceding chapter). In an essay on the narrative function he reintroduced this
hypothesis in connection with the difference between historiography (writing of history) and fiction, distinguishing between
two kinds of reference. As to the first he maintains that historical
narratives (historiography) refer to events outside the narrative
whereas fictional narratives do not. "But both historical and fictional narratives have in common an intersecting reference, a
reference to historicity, to the fundamental fact that we make
our history and are historical beings" (Ricoeur, 1978a:177). History gives a description in conventional language whereas fiction
gives a redescription, since it suppresses the first order reference
and refers in a second order. Both refer to human action: history
"through" relics, documents, and archives, and fiction by re-
describing reality. Thus, one cannot say that a literary work
(including a parable) is without reference. It is a work with a
split reference, that is, a work whose ultimate reference has as its
condition a suspension of the referential claim of conventional
language (Ricoeur, 1978a:194). He feels very strongly about the
referential claim of narrative discourse, albeit in the sense that
he understands the concept (cf. 186). It is a very important problem, since it penetrates to the very heart of one of the major
unsolved questions of literary criticism in general and New Testament scholarship in particular. It is of importance not only for
parable research but also for gospel research as a whole. We
shall return to Ricoeur's views, but let us first look at the problem from another angle.

The problem of reference has been described in literary criticism by likening texts to windows or mirrors (cf. Petersen,
1978a:20–21). Applied to New Testament scholarship Via writes:

> . . . one could say that the historical critic looks through
> the text to what it refers or points to [window–WSV] and
> treats the text as evidence for something else, while the
> literary critic looks at the text for what it says in itself
> by means of the patterning or shaping—the informing—
> of its content. (quoted in Petersen, 1978a:5)

To put it differently, what do the gospels or the parables of
Jesus refer to and how? The historical critic will probe the
growth phases of the text to establish "historical reality," whereas
the literary critic will look for referential relationships within the
text. As to the parables of Jesus, this problem has for a very long
time been described in terms of realism. Writes Dodd:

> In the parables of the Gospels . . . all is true to nature
> and to life. Each similitude or story is a perfect picture
> of something that can be observed in he world of our
> experience. The processes of nature are accurately
> observed and recorded; the actions of persons in the
> stories are in character; . . . It (sc. realism) arises from a
> conviction that there is no mere analogy, but an inward
> affinity, between the natural order and the spiritual
> order, or as we might put it in the language of the para-
> bles themselves, the Kingdom of God is intrinsically *like*
> the processes of nature and of the daily life of men.
> (1936:20–22)

Remarks such as these can be multiplied. Scholars like Dodd,
and especially Jeremias, did a tremendous job in unearthing a
vast amount of historical knowledge which reveals the background from which these stories arose. Thus, in their attempt to
"prove" the realism of the parables of Jesus, they provided us
with very useful material for creating a *frame of reference*
without which it would be impossible to read and validly interpret these stories. Who would have thought today that in ancient
Palestine they used to sow before they ploughed, as is told in the
parable of the sower (cf. Jeremias, 1970:7), to name but one of
the realities of the world in which Jesus lived?

At this stage we should remind ourselves of the aforemen-
tioned development in the interpretation of the parables as metaphors. It was said, amongst other things, that the parables are
open-ended and that a metaphor or parable ". . . is a bearer of
the reality to which it refers" (Wilder, 1971:84); stress was laid
on paradoxicality. Ricoeur (1975:99, 109, 112–18) speaks of the
extravagance of the parables. It was realized in the meantime

that "normalcy" (Crossan) only holds good for certain aspects of
the parables. There are numerous "atypical features" (Huffman,
1978) in the parables which can only be explained as literary
devices such as paradox and hyperbole. Let us take the parable
of the sower as an example. It occurs in Mark 4:3–8, Matthew
13:3–8, Luke 8:5–8, and the Gospel of Thomas 9. We have seen
that in Mark the threefold downward action is "balanced" by a
threefold upward movement. In view of the search for realism
the difference between the various versions regarding the *good
soil* has given rise to many discussions (cf. Carlston, 1975:139;
Crossan, 1980:40). The various versions read as follows:

> And some of the seed fell into good soil, where it bore
> fruit, yielding a hundredfold or, it might be sixtyfold or
> thirtyfold. (Matthew 13:8, *NEB*)

> And some of the seed fell into good soil, where it came
> up and grew, and bore fruit; and the yield was thirty-
> fold, sixtyfold, even a hundredfold. (Mark 4:8, *NEB*)

> And some of the seed fell into good soil, and grew, and
> yielded a hundredfold. (Luke 8:8, *NEB*)

> And others fell on the good earth; and it produced good
> fruit; it bore sixty per measure and one hundred and
> twenty per measure. (Gospel of Thomas 9 [82, 10], WSV)

On the basis of historical investigation it is maintained that a
tenfold yield amounts to a good harvest (cf. Crossan, 1980:41).
Scholars have nevertheless attempted to calculate exactly
whether the yield refers to the whole field (Jeremias, 1970:149)
or to the individual ears (Linnemann, 1961:149) and so on. The
harvest undoubtedly exceeds actual production, indicating that
realism is out of the question. What we have is hyperbole.
"God's harvest at the realization of the kingdom will be a more
productive one than a farmer ever reaped. This is revealed by
having this sower reap unrealistic amounts" (Huffman, 1978:
212).

The parable of the mustard seed has also been transmitted in
different versions. Unlike in Mark, in Luke 13:19 the mustard
seed ". . . grew to be a tree and the birds came to roost among
its branches." Traditionally the Markan version is preferred to
that of Q since it is more "accurate" in its description of the
mustard plant. However, the question is not whether it is more
or less correct. It is a matter of rhetoric. These two examples (of

which there are many: cf. Huffman, 1978) suggest that trying ". . . to put the 'camel through the needle's eye' literally, either by turning the former into a rope (Mark 10:25 . . .) or the latter into a pedestrian gate . . ." is rightly rejected as the work of unimaginative readers (cf. Huffman, 1978:220). His view is worth noting:

> I suggest that when Jesus spoke of hiring workmen at the eleventh hour, of a mustard seed that grew into a tree, of a farmer reaping a hundredfold, of a Samaritan offering to repay "whatever more you spend" on a Jewish stranger he made use of actor's skills *to convince his audiences.* (Huffman, 1978:220; italics mine)

The foregoing examples indicate a much greater hermeneutical problem, namely, the relationship between a narrative and its reference. If we say that biblical narratives represent reality, what do we mean? Is a parable a replica of reality, a representation of reality, an illustration of reality, an icon or symbol of reality? This type of question is important and will be dealt with below. First, I shall make a few observations about the character of the problem in the broader context of narrativity, namely, the Gospel of Mark. This is the text into which the parables under discussion are inserted. Besides, I would postulate that there is not a significant difference between the ways in which a parable and a gospel refer—both are "made up" stories, even if not the same genre.

I think it is correct to say that Mark made use of "real world" people to fill the narrative roles he created in his story of Jesus. The Pharisees are people who lived in Palestine during the life of Jesus. Jesus once lived in Galilee and so on; the places, customs, and cultural setting are equally realistic. The whole text is embedded in first-century Palestine. And that is why one has to know the language and the "real" world of the text. This does not, however, help us to answer the question of a text and its reference. What do the disciples in Mark, for example, represent? Ernest Best recently defined their "possible roles" in the following way:

> (1) They could signify themselves, the original disciples, no more and no less; this would be a purely historical position. Mark might approve of them or disapprove.
> (2) They could signify a group claiming to continue the

> position of the original disciples, and Mark might
> either favour or oppose the group.
> (3) They could signify some other contemporary group:
>   (a) the church as a whole, or (b) a part of the
>   church, e.g. its officials, or a group of heretics.
> (4) They could occupy a purely informatory role, i.e.,
>   Mark might believe that past history should deter-
>   mine the present and we should learn from the past.
>   (1977:379)

This example presents the problem of New Testament research
on the text and reference *in nuce*. The same phenomenon occurs
in Matthean research (cf. Luz, 1971) and throughout the narrative material of the New Testament. The most extreme form of
the problem is when the disciples in Mark are identified with the
so-called heretics in Mark's community; according to this view
Mark had to combat a heretical Christology (cf. Weeden, 1971;
Kingsbury, 1981). The following remark by Bultmann is only
partly true: ". . . a literary work or a fragment of tradition is a
primary source for the historical situation out of which it arose,
and is only a secondary source for the historical details concerning which it gives information" (as quoted by Marxsen, 1959:13).
Naturally the gospels tell us a lot about the world of their authors (cf. Polanyi, 1981b), but that does not mean that the text of a
gospel is somehow a reproduction of what actually happened.
The text of a gospel does not present a copy of reality. Mark's
gospel is not a replica of Mark's supposed community; it is a
narrative about the life of Jesus within some or other historical
setting. It is reality remade (cf. Goodman, 1968; 1978; 1981).

The objection may be raised that, since a gospel narrative
and a parable are two different text types, it is incorrect to talk
about their referential function as if they belonged to the same
type. Naturally one will have to keep in mind the metaphoric
nature of the parables. But parables are (metaphorical) *narratives*, and their narrative character is merely an example of
extended predication. Predication is given in narrative form.
Parables are by nature narratives, some of which occur in a
metaphorical context.

Despite the fact that parables are normally regarded as fictional stories or free creations ("frei erfundene Geschichten"),
there has been a consistent search for "realism" in the parables
or, to put it more positively, for making the horizons of reader
and parabolist meet. The things told in the parables are

undoubtedly related to first-century Palestine, but this does not imply that parables should be regarded as a report of "how things really happened." Anybody would concede that. In other words, although it is absolutely necessary for the interpreter of parables of Jesus to know exactly what "Samaritan" stands for, why the word refers to more than its meaning in a story by a Jew for Jews, it is just as important for him to know that a parable is a story. Narrative is the context of meaning of the parables. As fiction, that is, as "made up" stories, they are stories worth telling (cf. Polanyi, 1981b). Are they then so different from gospels which are also stories? Parables are stories in which reality is remade, even if in a metaphorical or some other—say, paradoxical—manner. Gospels are also stories in which reality is remade. Let us leave this problem for a moment and return to the problem of the referential aspect of parables.

To my mind the so-called open-endedness of metaphors has largely contributed to the definition of the referential function of parables as *redescription*. In the sense in which the term is used by Ricoeur it is nothing other than the open-endedness of metaphor, or the so-called priority of possibility as opposed to reality (cf. Jüngel, 1969). Redescription has to do with the world which is opened in front of the text (Ricoeur 1975:82) and not with that to which the text refers ("denotation"). To my mind Ricoeur and his followers, in their use of redescription, are not concerned with the same problem as the followers of Jakobson, with whom it is natural to speak of the referential function of the text as something purely internal or immanent. This one has to realize. Ricoeur's handling of the narrative function is too limited and his distinction between historiography and other kinds of narrative not convincing. Unlike Ricoeur I would say that even history (writing) is a "made up" story. Accordingly it would be simplistic to say ". . . only history may claim to address itself to events which actually happened, to actual deeds in the past" (Ricoeur, 1978:187). History is by its nature plotted; it is *poiesis* in the Aristotelian sense of the word (cf. Ricoeur, 1978a:192); it is reality remade. Cannot a historical novel also ". . . claim to address itself to events which actually happened . . . ," although on a different level? No doubt Ricoeur would agree to this. Should we not perhaps rephrase the problem as follows: how can history (writing) and novels, for example, be used to reconstruct "what happened?" The distinction

made by Scholes and Kellogg between empirical and fictional
narrative as used by Ricoeur is too broad to handle the problem
of the referential aspect of both parables and gospels as stories.
Are the characters, events, situations, and plots of gospels not
"imaginary" in the sense that they are the way the gospel writers
presented them, that is, *their* interpretations? Is a gospel "empirical" in the sense that it "may claim to address itself to events
which actually happened, *to actual deeds in the past*" (my
italics)? It is, in fact, empirical in the sense that it remakes the
deeds, among other things that actually happened, but it is not
because it does not reproduce the actual deeds of the past. The
characters, events, situations, and plots of gospel narratives are
not fictional in the sense that they are "frei erfunden," one may
say, but they also are not "empirical" in the above sense.
Although historians or biographers, for instance, work with facts,
the facts have to be evaluated and interpreted. Facts do not
automatically make the narrative, or render the meaning of the
narrative (Brooks and Warren, 1970:337). We should remind
ourselves that we are dealing with narrative discourse and avoid
the so-called "referential fallacy" of ". . . construing the signifier
alone as the sign and as referring directly to the real world
object without regard for the signified" (Petersen, 1978a:39).
Umberto Eco (1972:71) correctly says (a) "Man macht damit den
semiotischen Wert des Signifikans (sc. word, text) von seinem
Wahrheitswert abhängig;" and (b) "Man ist gezwungen, den
Gegenstand zu identifizieren, auf den sich das Signifikans
bezieht, und dieses Problem führt zu einer unauflösbaren
Aporie." There is a difference between a gospel and a parable in
that the gospel characters refer to characters who lived in Palestine during the first century, whereas those of parable stories
need never have existed at all. There might have been such a
person as the good Samaritan, but there is no reason why he
must have existed. This distinction is made not because of its
usefulness for describing the referential aspect of narrative but
only to draw attention to a difference between the two types of
texts, with due regard for the dangers involved in such a distinction between characters of a narrative.

The crux of the problem lies in the nature of narrative itself.
Narrative is the remaking of reality (= creating a *narrative
world*) through characterization, plot, and other narrative
devices. The storyteller creates a world of his own making with

its own time, space, characters, and plot, one which is called a "narrative world." Even if one were to be as true to the "real world" as possible in presenting part of it in narrative discourse, one will still be creating a "narrative world." And the resemblance between narrative world and real world cannot be seen as a one to one relationship, but as a remaking of the real world. In a sense this is what has been called *mimesis*: their significance is not the actuality of the events, but their logical structure (cf. Ricoeur, 1978a:192). Reference is to be analyzed not only with regard to the "real world" but, in the case of narratives, also with regard to the "narrative world." Narratives are not merely windows, nor are they purely mirrors: they are both. One could say that "disciples" in Mark refers to the original followers of Jesus, but one would immediately have to add how they refer and to what they refer in the gospel narrative. Mark's presentation of the disciples has to do with the narrative world he created. The answer as to how they refer is to be found in the way Mark created his narrative world. The same applies to parables.

Perhaps the distinction between representation as *mimesis* and illustration as *symbolic* (cf. Scholes and Kellogg, 1966:84) should not be applied to the parable story quite so readily either (cf. Tolbert, 1979:90). Even an exaggerated or a paradoxical story like the parable of the lost sheep can be "an attempt to create a replica of actuality" (= *mimesis*; cf. Scholes and Kellogg, 1966:84) in the sense of remaking reality. Parables are not patently symbolic or purely illustrative. They are stories of a specific kind. In parables reality is remade, often in an extreme form. If one is to ask how these stories refer, the answer would be: in the same way as other stories, that is, within their own narrative worlds. The following discussion by Nida of metaphors as icons (for example, speaking of a person as being a "pig," "wolf," or "rat") can help us a little further. "In reality," he says, "such metaphors are not necessarily based upon the true behavior of the objects which form the basis for the figurative meaning, but the figurative extension of meaning is based upon the way in which people regard such animals, irrespective of the actual truth of a situation" (Nida, 1981:20). The referents of signs with figurative meaning are *conceptual*. In this sense Ricoeur is correct in asserting that the first order referent (literal thing) is suspended and replaced by a second order referent (cf. Wittig, 1977). The redescription he is talking about is in fact the "narrative world" of literary criticism in the sense of reality remade, and not what he thinks it to be. Even a photograph cannot provide a copy of reality; it is a remaking thereof (cf. Goodman, 1978).

Because we do not have the objects, events, abstracts and so on of a "narrative world" at our disposal in the same way as we "have" those of the real world, it follows that opinions will differ greatly about what they really are. In view of what narrative discourse is, namely reality remade, it is clear that the signs in a narrative refer internally within this remade reality. The referents of these signs are to be sought within the "narrative world" of the text, be it a gospel or a parable. The first order reference is suspended, in the words of Ricoeur, to make room for a second order—that of the narrative world. The implication is not that parables as "fictions redescribe what conventional language has already *described*" (cf. Ricoeur, 1978a:193) but that they describe in conventional language a remade reality.

It therefore becomes clear that the answer to the question of how narratives (including parables as extended metaphors) refer lies primarily in the nature of narrative. Reference is bound to the expression in which it occurs. To put it differently, the nature of reference depends upon the type of context, be it single words, sentences, or discourse. Parables as parables refer, within their own narrative world, and so do gospels. But parables, like gospels, originate from and exist within the real world. That is why there are relationships between the narrative world of a narrative discourse and the real world of which it is part.

Are parables as metaphors open-ended? From the perspective of the reception of a narrative text, it may be said that the text invites the reader to participate in the narrative world of that text. Since reality is remade, it offers new perspectives to the reader. The participation of the reader in the text is stimulated by the way in which the message is structured. It creates a new world of reference, namely, a narrative world. This is the redescription of which Ricoeur speaks.

How does the metaphorical character of parables influence their reference? The "kingdom of God" is the referent of the narrative message of parables in general. Like all other signs, the reference of parables depends on the environment of the parable. The direct environment of the predicate of parables is normally the kingdom of God. It is to that sign, which as a sign also refers to some referent, that parables refer. If we know what the sign "kingdom of God" stands for, we would know what is being said about what. This was shown above in the short discussion of Dodd's and Jeremias's interpretation of the parable of the seed growing secretly. It is not all that difficult to determine the meaning of "kingdom of God," but what it refers to is often an open question. The storypart of a parable, like that of any other narrative, has a referent (or referents) in its own narrative world. The narrative message of this narrative, however, has as referent the kingdom of God. To put it more specifically, if the narrative message of the parable of the sower is that, despite the small beginning, there will be an abundant harvest, then this message would refer to the kingdom of God where ". . . the kingdom is like what *happens* in the story" (Ricoeur, 1975:98). Parables refer as stories. In their metaphoric context the message of the story refers to the kingdom of God.

How do embedded parables refer? In our discussion of the parables in Mark 4 in the first part of this chapter, it was shown how the parables and parabolic sayings are not only inserted into the narrative but how they are actually integrated into the network of intersignification of a narrative text. An attempt was made to give a brief survey of the place of Mark 4 in the narrative world of the gospel. It has become clear that these parables became an integral part of the complete narrative and its narrative world. Within the context of the characterization of the disciples as insiders as opposed to outsiders, these parables have to show, so to speak, how the kingdom is a mystery to the insiders and hidden from the outsiders. Because they are used in a context, they refer within that context. The narrative world of the gospel is the world within which parts of these stories in turn refer. In my view this clarifies the importance of *logos* and kingdom of God. These metaphorical stories and statements contribute to the meaning of Mark in a distinctive way. They are stories as communication and contribute to the meaning of the macronarrative.

Embedded parables and parts of such parables have referents in the narrative world of the text into which they are inserted.

*   *   *   *   *

In conclusion, let us consider a few things which have emerged from current research on parables. First, parable research in New Testament scholarship is normally conducted with a view to the parables of Jesus, that is, the historical Jesus. The importance is easily understood. In addition it is normally argued that parables should be interpreted according to their referent—the kingdom of God which is in turn interpreted in terms of the eschatological preaching of Jesus. This too follows naturally. In the third place, much is made of the fact that the parables of Jesus can be studied in groups, for example, tragic and comic parables; parables of advent, reversal, action; parables of growth, servants, and so on, emphasizing that various parables have a "common" theme. The usefulness of this approach is also self-evident. Furthermore, it has often been argued that context is a very important aspect of the parables of Jesus. Recently New Testament scholars have reached consensus about the form of the parables. As we have said repeatedly, Jesus' parables are spoken of in terms of metaphoricity, narrativity, and para-doxicality (and brevity). All these aspects, however, are empha-sized with regard to the parables of Jesus in their original form and meaning.

This approach poses at least two problems. First, there is the fact that little or no attention is paid to the problem of the conti-nuity or discontinuity between the oral and literary phases of the tradition of Jesus. In the above study some of the implications of the recording of Jesus' parables in a macro-text were pointed out. This is another facet of parable research, not the only but nevertheless an important one, which should receive much more attention than has hitherto been the case. Secondly, there is the problem of historical reconstruction. It is well-known that we can reconstruct the *Sitz im Leben* of the parables with some cer-tainty, but that from the sources at our disposal it is impossible to reconstruct the historical situation in which Jesus uttered a specific parable. This is a major problem which we will have to face sooner or later. The original parables may be considered stories as communication (cf. Polanyi, 1981b). Jesus most proba-bly told these stories not for their intrinsic worth but because he wanted to say something to his followers *about* some point raised in his conversations with them. It is commonly held that this something *about* which he told his parables was the kingdom of God. That is probably correct. But in his talks with his followers, various reasons could have given rise to such stories, not only as illustrations but as a means of communicating something about a topic that cropped up in their conversations. These reasons, these contextual settings in the life of Jesus, have been lost and cannot be reconstructed. Tolbert (1979:49) correctly maintains: "Unless historical criticism can supply a much more *specific* picture of the historical Jesus or the particular situation in which the parables were first told, historical interpretations of the parables will diverge as widely as modern philosophical or psychological interpretations. . . ." That is why it is so difficult to make comparative studies of the parables in their gospel contexts and in their context in the life of Jesus.

Even more important than the problems of what parables mean and to what they refer is how they mean and how they refer. If we can answer this question we will know the solutions to the other as well.

3

Reference: Reception, Redescription
and Reality

Bernard C. Lategan

Introduction

In the preceding chapter, Vorster comes to the conclusion
that "parables refer as parables within their own narrative
worlds" (61). In doing so, he highlights an important aspect of
reference. His conclusion is built on a wide variety of arguments. Most of these are convincing, while we shall return to
others in due course. However, what must be clear from the
outset is that Vorster is talking about reference in a specific and
restricted sense. He confines himself to "immediate" reference,
that is, to the first answer that can be given to the question:
"*about* what is the parable (or statement)?" In this study it will
be argued that reference functions in a much wider context.
This wider context has an important role to play when determining the more immediate reference of a story or statement. What
is meant by this will be discussed under three headings, namely,
text and reception, text and redescription, and text and reality.

Text and Reception

Until quite recently, the main thrust of research on the theory
of textual interpretation was in the direction of text-production
and text-transmission. If we keep the simple communication
model in mind:

$$\text{SOURCE} \longrightarrow \text{MESSAGE} \longrightarrow \text{RECEPTOR}$$
$$(\text{TEXT})$$

the focus was on the left-hand side and on the center of the diagram. The historical approach with all its variations was mainly

interested in the source and circumstances of origin, believing
that these aspects hold the key to the understanding of the text.
Studies in the structuralist mold concentrate on the center of the
diagram, that is, on the text as "work," analyzing its structure on
various levels, using mostly a text-immanent approach. Recently,
attention has shifted to the righthand side, with a whole series of
studies investigating the reception of texts (cf. Schmidt, 1975;
1980; Bürger, 1977; Grimm, 1975; 1977; Jauss, 1974; 1975; Iser,
1974; 1976; Zimmermann, 1974; Steinmetz, 1975; Naumann,
1975; 1977; Frey, 1974; and Hohendahl, 1974, for more details).
It is being realized more and more that an adequate theory of
(textual) communication must give acount of the process of
reception (cf. Schmidt, 1975:403, who distinguishes the three
components of literary communication as text-production, text
mediation, and text-reception).

The focus on reception has opened a number of new avenues
of investigation. It has led to claims like that of Schmidt that a text
has as many meanings as it has readers (1980:534) and to the
attempt by Jauss (1974) to use reception as a norm for evaluating
the literary quality of a work. This led to some interesting questions: Why does the popularity of a certain book fluctuate with
successive generations of readers? Why were certain "world
classics" a failure at the time of their first reception, but gained
recognition at a later stage? Can reception be a criterion to distinguish between art and kitsch? Does the "average reader" or the
critic determine the artistic value of a work?, and so on.

It is doubtful whether reception can function as a normative
indicator in any way. Nonetheless, the investigation of this phenomenon has underlined at least three aspects which have implication for the problem of reference:

> *Communication is not complete until the text has
> reached its final "destination."* Reception should there-
> fore be part of any theoretical reflection regarding the
> process of interpretation. This means *inter alia*—to refer
> to an issue Vorster has raised—that the problem of mul-
> tiple meaning and multiple interpretations cannot be
> solved by opting for the first and ignoring the latter. The
> phenomenon of multiple interpretations has specific
> implications for the understanding of reference, as we
> shall presently see.
> *Reading is not merely a reproductive, but essentially
> a productive activity.* Although this was already stressed

by Gadamer (1975:280), reception aesthetics has brought
forth many new aspects. For Iser, the literary work has
two poles—the artistic and the aesthetic. The artistic
refers to the text created by the author, the aesthetic to the
realization accomplished by the reader. "From this polar-
ity follows that the literary work cannot be completely
identical with the text, or with the realization of the text,
but in fact must lie halfway between the two" (1974:274).
But if the work is left to oscillate halfway between these
poles, further questions arise: who is the dominant figure
in the reading process—the writer trying to impose his
point of view on the reader via the text or the reader who
is free to create his own version of the text? According to
Sterne (cf. Iser, 1974:275), the text is something like an
arena in which reader and author participate in a game of
the imagination. The author must be careful not to under-
or over-play his hand. If he gives too little information and
stimulus to his reader, the latter is unable to respond. If he
gives too much and leaves nothing to the imagination, he
may also lose the attention of his reader. The interaction
between writer and reader is therefore stimulated not only
by the written, but also by the "unwritten text"—that
which is not stated explicitly but is, nonetheless, present
and active in the situation of communication.

What has all this to do with reference? It is important to give full recognition to the intersubjective nature
of textual communication. Reference cannot be analyzed
merely in terms of the world of the text—the world of
the reader as presupposed by the text must also be taken
into account. In doing so, we are not repeating the "referential fallacy" on the side of the author in the form of
a "reception fallacy" on the side of the reader, thereby
making an absent or undeterminable reader the criterion
to decide to what the text is referring. Just as the intention of the author can only be determined in terms of
his text, so the text constitutes the basis for analyzing the
anticipated reception by the reader. (We shall discuss
the distinction between the implied and real reader in
the following paragraph.) Reference inwards to the
world of the text presupposes a reference outwards to
the reception by the reader.

*The third aspect highlighted by reception is the
complex or "layered" nature of textual communication.*
Although illocutionary texts can function in a very
direct way ("Run!"), the line of communication is usually an extended one. This is especially true in the case
of biblical texts where our reading is in any case not the
first reception of the text. In literary criticism it has long
been accepted that a text may have whole generations of

readers besides the original reader(s) for whom it was
initially intended. The way in which the text is structured offers many clues for recognizing its "implied
reader," for delineating the audience to whom it is
addressed. The "real reader" of the text may differ con-
siderably from its "implied reader." Sometimes the
"implied reader" is explicitly identified, as in the case of
Luke 1:1, where the gospel is addressed to "Theophilus"
(although who this Theophilus was remains unclear);
sometimes it is to be inferred from indications in the
text, as in the case of the Gospel of Mark.

But even more important than revealing how the text is
built up in various layers, the implied reader becomes the route
by which the author reaches for the heart of the real reader. The
implied reader represents the response the author is aiming at or
assuming on the part of his audience. In this sense it functions as
a heuristic device to uncover the meaning of the text. It is a theoretical construct to gauge the intended effect of the text. The
implied reader is on the receiving end of all the various
indicators of the text. He experiences the full impact of all the
strategies employed by the author, integrates the various elements, and projects the ideal response to the text, that is, a
response congruent with the designs of the author as expressed
in the text.

The implied/real reader finds its counterpart in the im-
plied/real author. The real author as a historical figure, writing
at a certain point in history and working within a specific cultural and sociological context, has for a long time been the focal
point in the quest for understanding and interpreting texts. This
has especially been the case with studies in biblical literature, as
the history of exegesis testifies. The implied author is primarily a
textual concept. It can be described as "a textguided image of
the author" (Wuellner, 1981:66, Iser, 1980:69), an image built up
by an intricate network of numerous literary devices and
strategies. By means of the implied author major "values" are
established in the mind of the (real) reader. Wuellner (1981:28–
31) shows how in the story of Lazarus (John 11:1–57) one set of
values concerning life and death, revelation and its meaning,
belief and unbelief is set off against another set of values
attached to these topics. These values are patiently built up step
by step—Jesus' apparent unconcern with Lazarus' critical condition (John 11:4–7), his certainty that it will not end in death

(11:4)—although he is the first to confront the bystanders with the reality of their friend's death (11:14). This apparently paradoxical attitude towards death is paralleled by Jesus' unconcern regarding his own safety and possible death at the hands of the Jews (11:7–9). His evaluation of life and death is echoed by the prophecy of the high priest that it is better than one man should die instead of having the whole nation destroyed (11:50; notice the evaluatory term συμφέρει). It is exactly the ambiguity of this statement which provides the basis for two completely different evaluations of his death. In the case of Jesus, it is linked to the concept of the resurrection (11:25) and the implied author leaves little doubt what line he expects his readers to take. In a similar fashion two concepts of belief and unbelief are developed (11:13, 25–26, 40, 45) and two possible interpretations of his signs are established (11:4, 33, 37, 40, 45–48). John 11:44 provides a remarkable illustration of how strong the hand of the implied author can be in shaping the direction of the text—no interest whatsoever is shown in the person of Lazarus after his remarkable experience, no word is reported of what he said or did. The focus is immediately shifted to the reaction of the Jews and the Pharisees (11:45–46).

Despite the extent of its influence, the implied author is discernable in the text only in an indirect way and often operates on a subconscious level. Much more visible are the strategies employed by the implied author to direct his reader's attention. One of the most prominent of these devices is the use of the narrator. As far as the Gospel of Mark is concerned, Vorster (1980a:116–19; 1980b) has shown the important role of the narrator in structuring the gospel, in using a specific "point of view," in varying the time mode (*erzählte/besprochene Zeit*), in supplying additional information to the reader and commenting on the development of the story. In the case of the Lazarus story, the comment of the narrator becomes evident at various transitions in the narrative. In 11:12 the seemingly causal remark about Mary, identifying her as the woman who anointed Jesus' feet, has an important function: it is the first reference to Jesus' own burial and an indication that the Lazarus episode must be understood against Jesus' own death. In 11:13 a further comment by the narrator strengthens the development of the story in this direction. In 11:51–52, the deepest implication of Jesus' death is spelled out by the narrator.

The arsenal of weapons the narrator has at his disposal is impressive. Besides the variety of perspectives that can be achieved by shifting the point of view (cf. Vorster, 1980a:117), characterization offers numerous possibilities. Vorster has dealt with these in his analysis of Mark (1980a:126–30). To this may be added the possibility of "round" and "flat" characters (Wuellner, 1981:9). Flat characters have very few traits and their behavior is therefore predictable; in the Lazarus story the disciples and the Jewish authorities are examples of this type. Round characters are much more complex and often act in an unexpected way: Jesus, who tarries for two days instead of hurrying to his friend Lazarus's side when he receives the news of his critical condition (John 11:6), who does not share the fear his disciples have for his own death (11:8–9), who is apparently powerless to change the course of events (11:32,36) but then brings Lazarus back to life; Martha, who initially is confident that Jesus will change matters (11:229) but whose faith fails her in the face of the harsh realities of life (11:39); and of course Lazarus, whose change of condition is the most dramatic. Elsewhere I have referred to the phenomenon of change in the roles of characters and its function in furthering the narrative development (Lategan, 1978a:82). In literary texts, characters are first and foremost artistic constructs. In biblical material, this holds true also for certain genres, most noticeably the parables. In more historical material, the question of the relationship between the real and the fictional immediately comes to the fore—which is of course another form of the problem of reference. In the last section we shall return to the question of fictionality in biblical texts.

Another device used by the narrator is shifts in time and space. Besides the variations between *erzählte* and *besprochene Zeit*, the natural time sequence can be altered. Temporal indicators are to be found on various levels in the text. We can distinguish between "story time" and "discourse time." The former is the natural order of events presupposed by the story. These events, however, can be rearranged either by the author himself (flashback or anticipation of coming events is a well-known literary and cinematic device) or via one of the characters in the plot. In John 11, vv 18–20 represent such a rearrangement of events. According to v 17 Jesus is already in Bethany. Verses 18–20 return to what happened before his arrival, while v 21 resumes the main narrative.

Genette (1980:34) refers to "reading time" as a further distinction. By this is meant the time required by the reader to integrate the various temporal indicators of the text and to construct the time sequence of events. Certain events will be anticipated at the beginning of the text, others will become clear only in the light of subsequent information.

In a similar way "story space" and "discourse space" may be distinguished (cf. Wuellner, 1981:5–8). The list of literary and linguistic devices that can be used for structuring and shaping the text is seemingly inexhaustible. It varies from simple syntactic indicators like conjunctions and particles through changes in mood and perspectives to involved literary figures like metaphors and parables, with their accompanying features of transformation, topicalization, foregrounding and extra-patterning, interaction between tenor and vehicle, and so on (cf., e.g., Link, 1979; Genette, 1980; Wuellner, 1981:66; Maartens, 1980). Every change on the level of the signified is accompanied with a corresponding change on the level of the signifier. In this way the interplay between linguistic and literary elements can theoretically be accounted for (cf. Maartens, 1980), but a fruitful link with ancient (and modern) rhetorics also becomes possible (cf. Nida, et al., 1983).

The author therefore has a whole bag of tricks at his disposal. And he uses them—with a greater or lesser degree of efficiency—to cajole, to lead, to impress, to tempt, to shock, to exasperate, to assure, to persuade, to please his reader. In short, the virtuoso of the word uses every technique with one goal in mind: to communicate with his reader, to entice him to get involved in the possibilities opened by the text. Textual communication therefore is a cooperative enterprise. Author and reader stand in a "chiastic" relationship to one another: the implied reader is a construct of the real author, and the implied author is a construct of the real reader. The first is necessary to prepare the expected response to the text, the latter is a textguided image in order to get a grip on this intended response. The one presupposes the other and the mediation between the two is effected through the medium of the text. In a model designed for literary communication, Hernadi has shown how the rhetorical axis of communication is inevitably bound up with the mimetic axis of representation (1976:381). The text forms the meeting point

where the movement from the world as reservoir of signs to the
world as representable by signs runs across the line which moves
from the world as source of motivation via the real/implied
author to the implied/real reader, to the world as field of action.
Communication by means of verbal signs becomes possible
because of the referential potential of the text.

In guiding and nudging his reader, it is possible for the
author to steer him away from "reality" towards a self-contained
world created by the text. There is an element of "escapism" to
be found in all literature (Iser, 1974:284). In some texts this
becomes the dominant feature. The object is to entertain for its
own sake and shield the reader from extratextual realities. Despite all the similarities with literary texts, at this point biblical
texts reveal a distinct difference—the movement is consistently
in the opposite direction. Whatever strategies the author uses to
construct the "inside" of the text, the aim is to provide the
reader with a new perspective on extratextual reality. In the case
of the Lazarus story, the goal is to show Jesus for what he really
was, the one who is coming into the world (Wuellner, 1981:66),
and to affirm the need for believing in him. Vorster (1980a:131)
argues that the goal of Mark is to get and keep his readers
involved in Jesus as the Son of God (a recurring and linking
theme in the gospel), which, at the same time, implies *Nach-
folge* of Jesus. The movement is inexorably *outwards* towards
the "reality" which forms the background of the text and the
"reality" within which the reader finds himself. The question of
reference is therefore forced upon us. Although the world of the
text enjoys a relative autonomous existence, this may be decep-
tive, because its very existence is made possible by and depends
on the accompanying context from which it arose, which forms
a link with the context of the reader in terms of shared codes
and shared experience. The interaction between text and context
forms the wider framework within which communication takes
place (cf. Wuellner, 1981:35). In our discussion of the reciprocal
relationship between author and reader, we saw how the implied
author acts as link with extratextual realities, establishing specific
"values" in the text—values which reflect or are related to the
context within which the text functions. The implied author
therefore is of utmost importance for the question of reference.
On the "chip" of the text, which has its own internal circuitry (to
borrow a metaphor from present-day electronics), the implied

author forms the outside terminal which links up with the extratextual aspects to which the text is referring.

However complex the nature of the text, its various layers
and internal structure, the bottom line still remains: the function
of the text is to link real author with real reader in terms of the
real world in which they find themselves.

Text and Redescription

Let us take a different tack and rephrase the question of reference. Consider the last statement of the previous section. We
have already said something about the real author and the real
reader. But what is this "real world" in which they find
themselves? Is it the world as seen by the author, or as experienced by the reader? Or is it the world created by the text? In
other words: What happens to reference when inter-subjective
communication is objectified in the form of texts?

Inscripturation does affect several aspects of verbal communication. The difference between oral tradition and written documents has long since been a focal point in the discussion
regarding the interpretation of biblical texts (cf. Güttgemanns,
1971b:67–68; Ricoeur, 1975:67; 1976:35–37). It is clear that oral
and written material cannot be treated in the same way. While
oral communication is characterized by flexibility and open-
endedness, that is, the retention of various possibilities of execution, inscripturation implies the molding of the message in a
specific form. Syntactic and semantic relationships become fixed
and cannot be altered at will. Genre, point of view, minor and
major stylistic features—all imply a definite choice to the exclu-
sion of other possibilities.

The fixation of relationships by means of the text can be
viewed in either a negative or a postive light. Negatively, it may
be seen as restrictive, confining the message to one form at the cost
of other alternatives. It may be understood as signifying (historical) distance and therefore alienating in its effect. (This is one of
the main presuppositions of the historical method as applied to
biblical material). On the other hand, it may also be interpreted
positively as an essential step in preserving the message to be com-
municated. In Chapter 1, we referred to Ricoeur's arguments in
favor of inscripturation. It not only preserves the message because
of its structure, but also makes it transferable insofar as the text is

not bound to its situation of origin but free to travel forward in time. Furthermore, the publication of the text means exactly that the text is made public, becomes accessible to others, and forms the basis on which any claim or argument concerning the interpretation of the message must be based. In this sense the text marks out the battlefield on which the struggle for verification and validity of interpretation is to take place. As such it becomes the object of research and analysis.

We can go one step further. The text not only represents a certain permanency of relationships and not only enjoys a certain autonomy as published object: in it is compressed a whole world. In it a profusion of connecting lines from all directions finds its meeting point. Because of its highly concentrated nature, Wimsatt has talked about the "iconic solidity" of the text (1954:231). Language, says Ricoeur (1978b:225), takes on the thickness of a material or a *medium*. Because of this "density," the text becomes a work, a thing.

The existence of the text as concrete object, as a fixed structure with a "timeless" quality, cannot be ignored. This has implications for the way in which the text is to be analyzed and for the validation of any proposed interpretation. However, the "solidity" of the text may be misleading. It can obscure the fact that it forms part of a whole *movement* of communication. Traces of this movement are to be found in the text itself. It flows in two directions— towards the "inside" and towards the "outside" of the text. The text is the product of a centripetal force in which the communication event is compressed into a mere string of words. The contraction resulting in the text can be achieved by various means. One possibility is the technique of embedding, to which Vorster also refers. By creating "a story within a story," embedding can be seen as an encircling action by which one story is surrounded by another, thereby limiting the possibilities of the former. The text itself marks the points where such framing takes place: "He said;" "Once upon a time;" "The Kingdom of God is like. . . ." Embedding can assume very intricate forms. In some cases we do not find a mere repetition of the story, but the reaction of the audience to the original telling is incorporated in the retelling. New information is added or the narrator comments on the course of events. Formerly, *Traditionsgeschichte* tried to trace the course of venerable traditions, like the Abraham story or the Sinai traditions, through their various stages of retelling. Recent research on literary and narrative techniques has enabled us to understand the phenomenon of embedding better. For example, when previous receptions of a message have an influence on the shaping of subsequent retellings, we see the development of very complex and concentrated structures. In Chapter 1, I called these structures "enriched texts" and used the example of Matt 12:3–4, where a threefold reception of the Mosaic law is telescoped into a single text (15–16). Foreshortening the perspective in this way can cause confusion with regard to the referential function of the text. In Matt 12:3–4 at least three levels of reference are possible: David's understanding of the law in the original situation of his flight; Jesus' reference to David's interpretation, presupposing the traditional Mosaic understanding; and, lastly, Matthew's presentation of this episode to his readers. The three subjects imply three "worlds" of reference. The easy answer to this problem is that whatever the world of embedded characters may be, we are only dealing with *one* text, the final one, and any claims to reference or interpretation must be made in terms of the text in its present form. This answer is, of course, not completely satisfactory, because reference in the final text functions *by virtue* of the previous receptions. These previous receptions, each with its own "world" or frame of reference, are presupposed in the final text and form the foil against which the final text sets itself off.

Perhaps a reference to the physical properties of light may be illuminating. Van Peursen (1972:112) uses this illustration from physics to explain the ability of the text to combine quite diverse time sequences in a single structure and to relate these to one another as though they belong to the same level. Because of the speed with which light travels, there is a time difference between the position of an object at any given time and our observation of that position. When we look at stars and their constellations, we are in fact looking into the past: what we see are the positions assumed by stars hundreds and even thousands of years ago. Furthermore, from our perspective events from widely differing moments in time are observed simultaneously, as though they stand in direct relationship to one another. This synchronic perspective, this "cross cut" on the latitudinal axis, is developed further by Van Peursen in his concept of "dwars-tijd" (112). By this he means not only the relationship between various elements at a given point in time, but also their relation to the observer of these elements and to the *time* of his observation.

All the different trajectories of time converge in the moment of observation. When this "observation" is translated into the form of a text, the text inherits the same synchronic dimensions and the same complex and concentrated nature.

As we have seen, it is this concentrated nature which lends a "solidity" to the text and makes its existence as a concrete object possible (see above). But it easily can give rise to the further mistaken idea that the text possesses some kind of "metaphysical" status—that is, because it represents some form of abstraction it is one or more steps removed from "reality." The text, so it is argued, has no direct ties with reality but at most represents an "Abbildung" of reality, which in some cases stands in direct contradiction to reality. Again, an illustration from physics is useful. When we see the sun setting and at a certain moment touching the horizon, we do not observe "reality." Because of the time needed for the light of the sun to reach our eyes, we are in reality observing the position the sun *had* assumed some eight minutes earlier. At the moment of observation, the sun is already below the horizon. We are observing the past, not the present. Arguing along this line, the text may be severed from the realities it is referring to and accorded a "metaphysical" status. it becomes only a *model* of reality. As such, it can be treated as a self-contained entity, analyzed and decomposed into its various elements, which in their turn can be switched around at will to form new configurations—all without recourse to the "realities" the model is supposed to represent.

The flaw in the argument is of course that reality cannot be severed from the observation of reality in this way. The radiation of light by the sun is not something added on to the reality "sun," but is part of that reality. The phenomenon that this radiation is subjected to a time interval is likewise a "reality." Finally, an individual's observation of the sun through time-governed radiation is also a reality in its own terms. Radiation in time belongs to the essence of the phenomenon "sun" (Van Peursen, 1972:122). It is only by an artificial restriction of reality to a certain moment in time—in this case, the exact instant a light ray leaves the surface of the sun—that it becomes possible to speak of "looking into the past." Within a certain scientific framework, this restriction may be meaningful or even essential. But on the same basis, "reality" may just as well be restricted to the moment the light ray emanating from the sun strikes the eye of the beholder, making "reality" a matter of the present.

This rather abstract discussion concerning the physical properties of light may seem far removed from the question of reference. However, it does serve to highlight two important insights. First, it underlines the time dimension which forms a constitutive part of reality, however "static" this reality may seem to be. Second, it may help us to understand the communicative nature of phenomena, in this case, of the text. The ability of the phenomenon to project itself, to resist any confinement to a specific time and space, lies at the root of the communicative process. For the student of physics, it may be meaningful to distinguish between "sun" and "ray of sunlight." To the ordinary beholder, the image of the sun *is* the sun. At the same time, the sun is "here" *and* "there." It exists only in its own "time profile," which may vary, depending on the position of the observer. In this sense, the relation to the observer plays a vital part in determining what the sun is. The sun does not exist apart from the light rays which communicate its existence to an observer. Outside of time and space, that is, apart from a network of relationships, it becomes meaningless to talk about the sun. The horizon within which the sun functions as a phenomenon thus includes dynamic communication processes. To put it differently: the concept "sun," when functioning meaningfully, implies its own communication (Van Peursen, 1972:123).

When we move from the phenomenon of the sun to that of the text, the communicative nature of the latter is so much more apparent. Despite its static appearance as a fixed structure of elements, the text in fact is part of a whole movement by which information is transferred and understanding made possible. At the same time, the text contains an important turning point where the flow of information is redirected. This happens when the centripetal inclination of the text is reversed to become a centrifugal force. The former represents the cocking of the spring, the latter the release of the built-up energy. We have already had some indication of where this turning point lies and how it functions. What we are dealing with is the "bridging ability" of the text. In more than one sense, the text stands "astride in two worlds." One example of bridging is the way in which an object can be both "here" and "there," as we have seen in the case of the sun. But there are also other strategies to be employed, which in every case implies *movement*. Embedding (and therefore retelling) is an important example. A few paragraphs earlier we referred to the limiting effects of this strategy, where one story is contained within the boundaries of another. But there is another side to this phenomenon: embedding is also a means of shifting one story to the context of another, thereby broadening its scope and increasing its referential potential. The mobility achieved by embedding is one form of movement to be found in texts. Another technique is that of the implied/real author and reader (Ricoeur, 1978b:224, talks about the split addresser and addressee). By differentiating between the real author, the implied author, and even between the narrator in his different variations, flexibility is achieved and the range of the text immediately increased. Alternating between a first- and third-person narrator not only makes it possible to shift the reader from one point of view to the other, but also creates room to execute these maneuvers successfully. The movement in the text is based on its ability to mediate between various perspectives and this prepares the ultimate mediation between author and reader. The mobility of the text therefore hinges on the possibility of "splitting"—not only of the addresser and of the addressee, but eventually also of the reference (Ricoeur, 1978b: 224, who here follows a suggestion by Jakobson).

By *split reference* is simply meant the ability of reference to function on two levels at the same time. The direct or first-order reference runs parallel to or is superseded by a second-order reference on a more removed level. The ambiguity inherent in poetical texts is perhaps the most basic form of split reference. But more specialized literary forms, like extended metaphors or parables, operate by means of a similar doubling of the referential function. Important for our argument is to realize that split reference does not mean the mere repetition or duplication of reference in a different format. As in the case of the author and reader (real and implied), a shift takes place whereby a new perspective is opened on the second referential level—a perspective which becomes apparent by virtue of the juxtaposition with the first order reference. In this way, a "re-description" of reality is achieved—a concept extensively developed by Ricoeur (1975: 85). In the last section, we shall return to the implications of this concept for the relationship between text and reality. Here we want to focus on the movement inherent in an operation of this kind. The movement is not only "forward," but also "sideways."

A conscious effort is made to step outside the immediate context, to leave the first-order reference. This step "sideways" is made in order to gain a step forward in the process of communication. The transfer to a second order of reference has as its goal opening a new perspective on the situation of the reader. The transition is usually clearly marked: "Once upon a time . . .," or "The Kingdom of God is like. . . ." The intention of all these signals is to achieve a "seeing as." In this sense the text is an optical instrument which the author offers the reader to ". . . read within himself" (Genette, 1980:261). Perhaps the best example is the introductory formula used by the Majorcan storytellers: "It was and it was not" (Ricoeur, 1978b:224). With one foot the story stands within the world of the reader, with the other it takes a step outside. First-order reference is suspended in order to create maneuvering space for a fresh approach.

Let us take a concrete example and look more closely at a story already mentioned in the first chapter, namely that of Nathan and David (2 Sam 12). The strategy which Nathan uses when he speaks to David after the death of Uriah is most revealing. The prophet does not dare to approach the king directly. He starts off in an oblique way: "There were two men who lived in the same town; one was rich and the other poor." This introduction signals a story and immediately removes it from the first-order context in which David finds himself. The unsuspecting king is therefore completely at ease. In fact, it is by this very distanciation that a personal identification becomes possible. "David was very angry with the rich man" (12:5) (David speaks of this fictive character as if he is a man of flesh and blood!). The king has to step outside his own world in order to gain a new insight into this self-same world. Then comes the dramatic announcement: "You are that man!" (12:7). It is important to notice that the embedded story of the rich and the poor man, which forms a perfectly self-contained unit on its own, only functions in this context because of the tacit identification of David with the rich man. Without this "outside" reference, the tension created by the parable would not exist and the point would be missed. In fact, without the presupposed outside reference, the story would never have been told in the first place. Vorster's insistence that parables refer as parables within their own narrative world holds water only in a very restricted sense. It is no doubt true that parables create their own internal worlds of reference and that it would be wrong to interpret these as referring directly to concrete historical situations. Nonetheless, although parables have their own internal integrity, they can only function as parables by virtue of an (indirect) outside reference. Without the latter, there would be no tension, no point, and parables would lose their usefulness. But because they presuppose a wider referential context, parables become one of the most effective vehicles of redescription.

But let us press this point even further and take an even more "referential" example. Valéry has described the dance, which travels nowhere, as the model of the poetic act (cf. Ricoeur, 1978b:224). As an art form, the dance certainly is a prime example of *art pour l'art*. It moves in a world of its own, apparently without any referential pretensions. The dance travels in a circle and indeed brings us nowhere but to the place where we started. And yet, in all cultures, the dance represents the most intense form of interpretation of the realities of life and one of the most suggestive vehicles for the redescription of reality. Even in the case of such an abstract form as the dance, the tension and interaction with a wider referential context remains esssential.

In the light of what has been said so far, Vorster's objection to Ricoeur's concept of the "world in front of the text" seems difficult to maintain. The background of this remark by Ricoeur is his rejection of the "always difficult and often impossible quest for an intention hidden behind the work" (1978b:220). By this he means the ideal of romantic hermeneutics to establish a complete harmony between the spirit of the author and that of the reader. Instead, he proposes a quest "that addressed the world displayed before the work" (1978b:220). In terms of our discussion so far, this would tie in with the redescription effected by the text, with the proposed world suggested by the text. Certainly, this proposed world comes into view as a second step, only after the first step of analyzing the text in its own terms has taken place. But we have also seen that the text in its own terms has taken place. But we have also seen that the text does not exist apart from its ability to communicate its own possibilities and to project these into the future. Is it possible then to talk of the meaning *in* a text apart from considering the meaning *in front of* the text? This distinction can only be provisional and temporary.

For the same reasons, the distinction between multiple meaning and multiple interpretations is valid and useful so far as it goes. But is does not solve our real problem because from our discussion is has become clear that meaning and interpretation in the above sense are structurally and semiotically related to one another. If we keep the semiotic triangle in mind

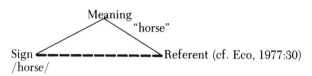

the *meaning* of the sign is the relatively easier question to answer and therefore it is represented with a solid line. Let us remember that this question can *only* be answered because of a shared experience—as clearly illustrated by Eco in his example (1977:28–29). The recognizing of the sign /horse/ depends on learning the *code* (e.g., teaching an Eskimo what /horse/ means by giving him a definition or by drawing a picture of a horse), but *also* on a "*Reaktionsneigung*," based on common experience (which leads the Eskimo to bring an actual horse or to neigh like one when a picture of a horse is shown to him). The relationship between sign and meaning becomes operative *only* when this shared experience exists, when this wider context of "reality" is presupposed.

The difficult question, as Vorster is well aware (cf. Chap. 2), is the relationship between sign and referent; in Eco's diagram it is therefore also indicated by a *broken* line. We have to do with special problems like the referent being absent or even non-existent in "reality"—cf. the well-known example of *unicorn*, which has both a sign and a meaning ("a one-horned animal"), but no referent in actual "reality." These are special cases which are all part of the basic question of the relationship between sign and referent, between language and "reality." It is not easy to find a completely satisfying answer, and certainly many problems remain unsolved (cf. below). The point we are making here is that these problems do not relieve us from the responsibility of searching for a clear as possible understanding of the relationship between the sign and its meaning, because,as our discussion so far has indicated, this relationship is closely related to the relationship between sign and referent or "reality."

All the indications of movement in the text, on all different levels and by all the various strategies, testify to the dynamic nature of the text. And so far as reference is concerned, all these different means serve the function of redescription. In concluding this section, the basic semiotic model will be used as a theoretical framework to explain the more complex phenomenon of redescription. The semiotic triangle illustrates exactly the *Umweg* which redescription (i.e., meaning by means of the sign and the rearrangement of elements in terms of a text) takes to link up again with extratextual reality.

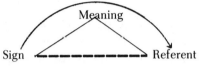

Meaning

Sign ◄— — — — — — —► Referent

The model can be expanded to:

redescription

= *meaning* as configuration of signs, rearrangement of reality in terms of the text.

text ◄— — — —► extratextual reality
(sign)   (*referent*)

The thrust of the movement remains toward the referent, and the tension lies between sign and referent. Even in cases of so-called zero-denotation (Ricoeur, 1978b:221), the implication of an extratextual reality is still there.

This is what Wuellner (1981:31) calls the context of the text, that is, all the people, all the things—all the existents—as pre-processed by the author's and the reader's cultural, literary, or everyday codes. As encoded items from extratextual realities, these existents function intratextually, but always in interaction with these realities themselves. Of course, the deictic functions are more direct in some texts than in others. But even the so-called self-contained texts can communicate only because of the underlying existence (although not explicitly expressed) of a relationship or tension between text and extra-textual reality, between sign and referent. "We belong to history before telling stories and writing history" (Ricoeur, 1978a:196). Reflection on the redescription achieved by the text as dynamic interaction leads us inevitably to the question of text and reality.

Text and Reality

From what has been said previously, it is clear that in any discussion of "reality" we are confronted with an extremely complex issue. The ontological problem has been a dominating theme since the earliest stages of western thought. It evolved through numerous phases, moving from a static to a more dynamic view of reality, sometimes temporarily disappearing from the scene (cf. Heidegger's accusation of *Seinsvergessenheit*) only to return in a new variation.

It was only natural that reflection on art, and especially literature, was influenced from the beginning by ontological precepts. Plato's views on the primordial status of ideas had direct consequences for his aesthetics. The artist's work represents a third level of abstraction, being a *Nachbild* of what is already an *Abbild* of the *Urbild* (Blumenberg, 1969:16). Aristotle's influence on subsequent literary theory was decisive, and his famous concept of *mimēsis* was the first attempt to clarify the relationship between literature and reality (cf. *Poetics*, chapters 2 and 3). Without intending to prolong "seemingly endless ontological discussions" (Wildekamp, et al., 1980:549), we shall touch on a few aspects of this problem to provide a background for our discussion of reference.

What is meant by "reality"? At first glance, the answer would appear to be self-evident, as everybody seems to be sure exactly what constitutes "the real world," what is "real" and what is not. But when we try to define it, reality proves to be very elusive. It soon becomes clear that we are not dealing with a fixed entity, but with a moving target. "Reality" is closely linked to an individual's frame of reference or "field of experience" (cf. Van Peursen, 1972:26), which, due to various factors, may shift from time to time and from situation to situation. Although there may be an overlap with other frames of reference, a complete consensus appears to be an unattainable ideal. It is therefore more satisfying to give recognition to this "individualistic" dimension of reality which is related to a specific frame of reference (cf. Goodman, 1978:20; Wildekamp, et al.,

1980:548). As far as texts are concerned, this would enable us to distinguish between various "realities" or "worlds"—that of the author, of the text, of the reader—which may or may not overlap to any given degree.[1]

As far as literary texts are concerned, the problem may be viewed from two perspectives: from reality to text and from text to reality. The former concerns the question: In what way do texts represent or reproduce reality? (Again, we are not dealing with a modern problem: the debate *pro* and *contra* nominalism was in essence concerned with the same issue). Even on the level of the sign, we are forewarned against identifying sign and reality. Insofar as the sign is something which stands for something else, identification is ruled out by definition. The sign is always a minimal unit, a a reduction of reality, which represents something from a specific perspective and not in its totality (cf. Eco, 1977:31). It is even more important to notice that the sign primarily expresses *relationships* between entities. In its most formalized form—for example, a mathematical formula—the *relational* dimension is most visible: A:B = C:D. Although the symbols may refer to any number of entities in "reality" and thereby remain "open" (posing the difficult problem of multiple meaning and/or interpretations), the relationship between the various symbols is fixed. The sign may have a dimension of resemblance (cf. the sign of the cross), but even then it is highly formalized.

When moving from the atomical level of signs to the more coherent level of texts, the feature of resemblance becomes much more prominent. Literary texts, for example, quite obviously represent reality in some way or another. We are dealing here with one of the basic and timeless questions inherent in all forms of art: In what way is art an *imitatio* of reality? The first answer would be that it evidently is not a *copy* of reality. But this holds true even for non-art forms of literature, such as historiography. Even when pursuing the goal of compiling a scientifically accurate report of what *exactly* has happened, restricting oneself to what can be verified historically, the result is not a

---

[1] Because we are dealing with texts we are leaving aside other possible variations of the concept "reality"—cf., e.g., Blumenberg, (1979:10–13), who distinguishes between a "Realität der momentanen Evidenz," a "garantierte Realität," reality as a "Realisierung eines in sich einstimmigen Kontextes" and a "Realität als das dem Subjekt nicht Gefügige."

reproduction of reality. By the very selection and arrangement of facts, by the specific point of view chosen, the report assumes—in spite of its scientific nature—features of a world of its own. Vorster is therefore right when objecting to a statement by Ricoeur that "only history may claim to address itself to events which actually happened, to actual deeds in the past" (Ricoeur, 1978a:187). Vorster points out that history itself is "reality remade" and that, on the other hand, a historical novel can also address itself to events which actually happened (Chapter 2). At the end of Chapter 1, I referred to the structuredness of history and to the historicity of any structure to make more or less the same point. However, in the end Vorster may discover more common ground with Ricoeur on this issue. It is Ricoeur's intention to show that any attempt to maintain a rigid division between empirical and fictional narratives, and to link this difference to a break between their respective truth-claims, is bound to fail (1978a:187). He himself wants to go beyond this superficial contrast in order "to overcome the apparent dissimilarity between true and fictional narrative at the level of reference" (1978a:188).

Be that as it may, the problems raised by working with categories like "empirical" and "fictional narrative" (which Vorster finds too broad a classification to be really useful) are indicative of the difficulty encountered when trying to draw a sharp line between fiction and nonfiction. What seems to be a self-evident and clearcut distinction in the beginning tends to become very fuzzy in the end. From the scientific historical report, to the autobiography with the author's perspective on specific events, to a biography with reconstructed episodes and inferred developments, to a historical novel with invented dialogue between historical personages, to a "period" novel, to a "frei erfundene Geschichte" with explicit or implied references to historical events or persons (*World War III, The Day of the Jackal*), to a fantasy world interpreting everyday experiences (*Alice in Wonderland, The Ring*)—along this line, the boundaries between fact and fiction are bound to become blurred. No wonder that works like Solzhenitsyn's *The First Circle* or *Cancer Ward* have been called "faction" (Shipley, 1970:119). Neither is it surprising that *Geschichtsähnlichkeit* became a valued characteristic of fiction, or that new labels like "nonhistorical realistic narrative" made their appearance (Kermode, 1979:121–23). Here we encounter the strange phenomenon that too much attention to realism in the end spoils the life-like effect created by fiction. A case in point is *Ulysses*, where the elaborate and minutely detailed descriptions supplied by Joyce constantly remind the reader that he is *not* dealing with reality, but with an illusion created by the author. On the other hand, Aristotle pointed out that fiction may approximate a general truth more closely than a particular and perhaps unique fact (*Poetics*, chapter 9). Goodman (1965; 1966; 1968; 1978) never tires of reminding us that fiction involves a remaking of *reality*. Interesting in this respect also are Caird's views on the value of fictitious narrative for the historian (1980:206). See also Traugott and Pratt's views on fiction and nonfiction (1980:259f.).

Are we to conclude that we are dealing with some strange form of chiasm—that the more realistic and detailed the account, the higher the illusory effect of the text, the more fictive the text, and the closer the approximation of a universal truth (e.g., *The Screwtape Letters*, and, for that matter, all forms of myth)? Tying a text to a specific moment or place in reality does, of course, restrict its range of applicability, in the same way that the individual realization of language as *parole* represents a limitation in comparison to the still free-floating possibilities of *langue*. Jauss (1974b:238) points out that there exists the same uneasy relationship between the aspects of *vrai* and *historique* in literary texts—being both contrastive and complementary at the same time.

It would seem that we are left with little choice but to accept the imprecise nature of the distinction between fiction and nonfiction with a grin and bear it. But there may be more to it than what meets the eye—the lack of clear boundaries may be indicative of a deeper kinship between the two types of literature. Ricoeur has drawn attention to the two functions of the verb, "to be"—what he calls the "is" of equivalence and the "is" of determination (1978b:248). Too often the former is read where the latter is intended. The former is used to identify, the latter to describe. While the former presupposes equivalence, the latter fulfills the function of a simile (is/like). The former is based on congruence between subject and predicate; in the case of the latter, the boundaries no longer overlap completely but a shift has taken place. When this difference is not respected, mistakes will happen, like reading a biblical text as if equivalence in historical matters is

intended. But it is not only a case of mistaken identity—both functions of the verb "to be" may act simultaneously. This duality not
only explains the kinship between fact and fiction, but forms the
basis of all metaphorical speech. It is the combination of an "it
was" and an "it was not" which sets the referential process in
motion and which makes redescription possible. For this reason,
Ricoeur is able to maintain that history is both a literary artifact
and a representation of reality (1978a:191). So the question of the
relationship with reality remains.

There have been several, some even drastic, attempts to
eliminate the tiresome problem of reference. For example, in
order to avoid "highly complicated and seemingly endless ontological discussions," Wildekamp, et al. (1980:549) develop an
idea of Goodman (1969:21) and define "fictionality in terms of
labels having null denotation and not in terms of non-existing
objects." Although this kind of distinction may be useful for the
empirical research they are conducting, it avoids rather than
clarifies the problem we are interested in. Eco (1977:154–57) dis-
cusses the quite different approach adopted by Strawson
(1971:7). He draws a sharp line between the *meaning* and the
use of an utterance. The former, in the sense of the signifíe
(Signifikat), refers to the meaning of an utterance *in abstracto*,
that is, outside a situation of actual language usage. In such a
"suspended" state, the utterance is subject to a certain set of rules
which would allow sentences like "The King of France is wise"
but disallow "The King of France snowed last night"—because
of the semantic selection restrictions built into the concept
"snow." In actual usage, a different set of rules comes into play
which makes it possible to verify the first statement empirically
(depending on which king of France is meant), and which
would definitely make a sentence like "The present king of
France is bald" false if uttered in 1980. The idea is that
semiotics should confine itself to *meaning* in the above-
mentioned sense and exclude the contingencies of concrete language usage as object of its methodological reflection. This line
of thought has substantially influenced subsequent developments
in both analytical philosophy and linguistics. Kempson (1977:58–
74) shows how the whole debate between a "speech act semantics" and a "truth-conditional semantics" hinges on the question
of whether word or sentence meanings should be considered *in
vacuo* or whether the conditions for actual use should be part of

any reflection on semantic theory. The new interest in pragmatics is a direct consequence of these developments.

The attempt to exorcise the ghost of reference (Eco, 1977:157) is bound to fail for at least two reasons. Firstly, the field of meaning cannot be sealed off hermetically from concrete usage, as new contexts can be devised continually which would make sense of even such nonsensical utterances (in logical terms) as "The king of France snowed last night." Secondly, and more importantly, words like "present" in the example mentioned ("The *present* king of France") are indices or "pointing finger-words" which defy any restriction to semiotics and which inexorably lead the movement from the text to reality. "Der Index dient zur konkreten Bezugnahme, *steht* also nicht *für etwas*, sondern ist *zugleich* mit diesem anderen da, und das bedeutet, dass ihm eines der Charakteristika des Zeichens fehlt—oder, so könnte man sagen, dass er der einzige Zeichentyp ist, der kein Signifikat, sondern nur einen Referenten hat" (Eco, 1977:156–57).

Here we stumble on the limits of the semiotic process. The essential nature of the sign is that it stands for something else and, although this "something else" in its turn can become a sign and stand for yet a further signifié, thereby theoretically setting in motion a seemingly unending process of "semiosis" (Eco, 1977:162), this process stops in practice when sign and referent are simultaneously present in the moment of communication, as is the case in the example just cited in the previous paragraph. Van Peursen (1972) has argued extensively for a "deictic" ontology, whereby facts are understood not as static entities but as indicators of dynamic forces operating in the field of concrete human existence, depending on specific values. In this ontology, the concept "world" functions not as a substantive, but as a demonstrative (25), and language has a very strong *deictic* function. It becomes the vehicle by which the deictic nature of reality itself is preserved, but also the means by which it is unlocked.

The discovery of the deictic relationship between language and reality indicates that we have passed the turning point between the inward and the outward movement of communication in a text. At the beginning of this section, we started by investigating the inward leg, from reality to text, and now find ourselves considering the movement from text to reality. Kermode (1979) has built a strong case, as far as the gospels are concerned, for the priority of the text (and the necessities of the text) over against the events and, by implication, over against the reality referred to in the text. He shows, with a wide variety of examples drawn from the gospels, how freely the evangelists treat historical material in their narratives. These writers, he maintains, place a high premium on "followability" (113) in their stories, while the history-likeness of the gospels is a secondary effect consciously created by them. As Henry James pointed out, the novelist is obliged to maintain the fiction that his fiction is history (122). To defend the truth of their narratives, the evangelists did not hesitate to invent the events needed for the composition of the gospels as stories (109, 111, 114).

The position of Kermode is not unusual in biblical research. The whole concept of *vaticinium ex eventu* rests on the assumption that the necessity of proving a theological point is the mother of the invention of the required events. A case in point would be Wrede's explanation of Paul's christology. But Kermode does not give a satisfactory explanation of how this process is set in motion. Nor does he fully appreciate the secondary nature of the evangelist's interpretation. It is a commonplace that what we have in the gospels are not bruta facta, but already *interpreted* history (cf. Lategan, 1979:132). The meaning of events could be placed within different frameworks (cf. Caird, 1980:209–11, for examples from both the Old and New Testaments). Insofar as each of the gospels reveals its own narrative structure, Kermode is justified in referring to a narrative structure imposed on events (1979:117). But this process was set in motion by what the evangelists experienced as new and unique events: Jesus' life, preaching, death, and resurrection. The primary impulse behind the interpretation of Jesus' message and mission and the reinterpretation of the tradition were specific occurrences (cf. Lategan, 1973:97). This is what lies behind the christological reflection of the New Testament, the concept of a New versus an Old Testament (and the reappraisal of all previous Jewish tradition—cf. the exegetical presuppositions and conclusions in Hebrews) and the ongoing *Wirkungsgeschichte* of the Christian message. Instead of being a brainchild of a novelist, conceived under pressure from the demands made by his story, priority belongs to these primary events which swept in their wake a whole movement of reflection and which found its precipitation (inter alia) in the form of written documents. That these documents contain reinterpretation as a secondary stage of communication, and the individual earmarks of their authors, is only to be expected.

But what *is* preserved in these biblical texts? What is the "reality" of these seminal events, after all? If the *imitatio*-concept has proved to be untenable, the answer is to be sought in a different direction. Presupposing these events, the text preserves their essential relationships (A:B = C:D) with a view to future realization. It is in this sense that Ricoeur talks about the proposed world of the text that we may inhabit (1978b:244). It is precisely because of the persuasive powers of the narrative to depict a world which is familiar enough to recognize, but different enough to be inviting, that the evangelists use the narrative form. In doing so, the *mediating* role of language is utilized to its full extent. But, by opting for the narrative form, the evangelists are merely following the lead of Jesus, who not only made profuse use of the parable but also acted out in his own deeds the narrative of love, concern, and the ultimate sacrifice— thereby revealing (in a *deictic* and not merely informative way) the secret of life. It is this "Verhalten Jesu" (Jüngel, 1962:277, following Fuchs) which preserves the essential relationships and provides the base for a process of ongoing reinterpretation. The New Testament writers do not hesitate to switch to other forms of communication (epistle, apocalypse) when they continue this process and draw out the implications in new situations which require a further redescription. This is why Paul can preserve a balance between coherence and contingency in his letters (Beker, 1980:11–16). Working from a coherent center he meets the contingent needs of the developing and struggling churches. In this sense, all christological reflection can be understood as a redescription of the narrative acted and proclaimed by Jesus. To expect the text to duplicate or merely preserve the seminal events is to misunderstand the communicative nature of the text. From the reality of these events the text mediates their essential meaning to the reality of the reader (cf. the yes-and-no answer of Vorster in the preceding chapter, p. 59). This process takes place within the ongoing stream of history and is therefore open to historical investigation. However, historical research is needed not merely to pinpoint the process at a given point in time but to keep the future open. In this way, the contemporary reader can continue the narrative of the biblical text, lending to it a touch (and hopefully more) of reality in his or her own life and times.

4

Reader-Response, Redescription, and Reference: "You Are the Man" (2 Sam 12:7)

Willem S. Vorster

> . . . reading a text narratively (reading it 'for the story')
> means asking above all questions that have narrative rel-
> evance—questions generally referring back to the pro-
> airetic dimension and the story line—and finding
> answers to them. If attempting to read a narrative maxi-
> mally involves questions and answers about any and all
> of its meaningful aspects, reading it minimally involves
> questions and answers about what happens. (Price,
> 1982:110)

Notwithstanding the following remarks in connection with
reception, redescription, and reference of the parables of Jesus
above, Lategan finds my views on reference too restrictive and
limiting. I wrote:

> From the perspective of the reception of a narrative
> text, it may be said that the text invites the reader to
> participate in the narrative world of that text. Since
> reality is remade, it offers new perspectives to the
> reader. The participation of the reader in the text is
> stimulated by the way in which the message is struc-
> tured. It creates a new world of reference, namely, a
> narrative world. (cf. p. 62 above)

In his reaction to that essay, Lategan maintains that reference
should be related to all aspects of the communication act,
including sender, text, and receptor. In this way, he says, the
context in which reference functions is appropriately widened.
"This wider context has an important role to play when determining the more immediate reference of a story or statement"
(cf. p. 67 above). He argues that the referential status of a text is
not restricted to "what it refers to" immanently, or outside the

text (backwards), but also in front of the text.

To avoid unnecessary misunderstanding, and also to further our discussion, I have decided to analyze the story of Nathan and David in Samuel 12 with a view to reader-response, re-description, and reference. Lategan refers to this story twice in his two chapters above as a case in point. In chapter 3 he offers us his reception of the parable and its application (cf. pp. 67–93 above).

The thesis I wish to propound in this essay is the following: *The referential status of a sentence, or for that matter of a cluster of sentences like a story, is directly related to its semantic function.* An adequate response to what a text (a sentence, for example) refers to depends on its semantic function. It makes quite a difference whether a language unit is descriptive or non-descriptive (social, expressive, or instrumental; cf. Lyons, 1977:50). The thesis will be argued by (1) discussing different (modern) receptions of Nathan's parable and its application in 2 Samuel, and (2) by analyzing reception, redescription, and reference with regard to the story as embedded in 2 Samuel. In addition, the thesis will be worked out by discussing some theoretical aspects of the problem and applying them to the text under discussion.

Modern Receptions of Nathan's Parable

The story of David's affair with Bathsheba and the consequent rebuke by Nathan has captured the imagination of many a student of the Old Testament. The parable of Nathan and its application in the David, Uriah, and Bathsheba episode is most revealing when it is studied from the perspective of reception, redescription, and reference. It reads as follows (*NEB* translation):

> The Lord sent Nathan the prophet to David, and when he entered his presence, he said to him, 'There were once two men in the same city, one rich and the other poor. The rich man had large flocks and herds, but the poor man had nothing of his own except one little ewe lamb. He reared it himself, and it grew up in his home with his own sons. It ate from his dish, drank from his cup and nestled in his arms; it was like a daughter to him. One day a traveller came to the rich man's house, and he, too mean to take something from his own flocks and herds to serve to his guest, took the poor man's lamb

and served up that.' David was very angry, and burst
out, 'As the *Lord* lives, the man who did this deserves to
die! He shall pay for the lamb four times over, because
he has done this and shown no pity.' Then Nathan said
to David, 'You are the man. This is the word of the *Lord*
the God of Israel to you: "I anointed you king over
Israel, I rescued you from the power of Saul, I gave you
your master's daughter and his wives to be your own, I
gave you the daughters of Israel and Judah; and, had
this not been enough, I would have added other favours
as great. Why then have you flouted the word of the
Lord by doing what is wrong in my eyes? You have
struck down Uriah the Hittite with the sword; the man
himself you murdered by the sword of the Ammonites,
and you have stolen his wife. Now, therefore, since you
have despised me and taken the wife of Uriah the
Hittite to be your own wife, your family shall never
again have rest from the sword." This is the word of the
Lord: "I will bring trouble upon you from within your
own family; I will take your wives and give them to
another man before your eyes, and he will lie with them
in broad daylight. What you did was done in secret; but
I will do this in the light of day for all Israel to see."'
David said to Nathan, 'I have sinned against the *Lord*.'
Nathan answered him, 'The *Lord* has laid on another
the consequences of your sin: you shall not die, but,
because in this you have shown your contempt for the
Lord, the boy that will be born to you shall die.'

Even a cursory reading of 2 Samuel 12 makes it clear that
Nathan's parable and its application is a textbook example for
illustrating problems of the interpretation of ancient texts. A number of very important questions arise in connection with communication: Why did the communication between Nathan and David
first fail and eventually succeed? Is it because Nathan's story is
ambiguous, or is it because of David's expectation as a hearer that
he heard the story incorrectly? Why are both David's and
Nathan's hearings "possible"? Is it because stories are by nature
plurisignificant and for that reason open to multiple interpretations? Is it possible in principle that the story refers both immanently and to the extra-linguistic world, or, as Lategan would have
it, in front of the text, opening up a new possibility for David? All
these and many other questions arise when the text is read with a
view to reference and reader-response. We are in the fortunate
position of having two (narrated) hearings of the same story, the
one by a receptor (David) and the other by the sender of the story

(Nathan as interpreter, in his remark to David about the "correct" hearing of the story). The fact that the parable and its application are embedded in a larger text adds to the interest and complexity of its interpretation.

Nathan's parable and its application form part of the so-called "Succession Narrative" (*Thronfolgegeschichte*), generally taken to consist of 2 Samuel 9–20 plus 1 Kings 1–2. Hardly any other text in the Bible could better illustrate the influence which views on text type have on reader-response and reference. Although it is almost universally agreed that the *Succession Narrative* is a well-told story, it is certainly not its narrative characteristics which received the most attention or had the greatest influence on its interpretation. It was only recently that scholars started paying attention to the text as *narrative*. This is of direct relevance for our purpose, since classificatory tags like history, poetry, legend, parable, and so on tend to lead or mislead the reader.

In recent years (cf. Gunn, 1978:20) the *Succession Narrative* has been characterized as "history," "political propaganda," "wisdom" and/or "didactic literature," and also as "story, told in a traditional vein, as a work of art and entertainment" (Gunn, 1978:38). Some regard it as the beginning of historiography (cf. von Rad). "This document is Israelite history writing at its very best. As a result of this writer's historical scholarship, the last part of the reign of David is one of the best documented periods in the history of Israel" (Tucker, 1971:36). Although this view has not gone without challenge (cf. Whybray, 1968), it has influenced generations of scholars for whom the story as such refers backwards to events and persons outside the text. According to this view the semantic function of the story is descriptive. It describes persons in the real world, how they lived and what they did, and real events.

According to Rost (1926), however, the real concern of the story is with dynastic politics. It was written during the early years of Solomon's reign to propagate his glory. The theme is his succession. The Solomonic date obviously facilitated this reading. The purpose is to justify Solomon's succession. Together dating and purpose influence the meaning and reference of the story since it is related to a particular situation in the real world.

Taking his cue from the story of David and Bathsheba, Delekat (1967) argues for the anti-Davidic and anti-Solomonic

polemic of the narrative as a whole. Both anti- and pro-
propaganda trends discovered during the history of research
allegedly originate from different stages in the growth of the
story (cf. Veijola, 1975). This makes the problem of meaning
and reference a very complicated matter, because it becomes
almost impossible to know to which layer of tradition any part
of the final story refers, let alone the problems of semantic function and cohesion.

Whybray (1968:47) regards the *Succession Narrative* as a
political document, a novel "—albeit a historical one—rather
than a work of history properly speaking. No doubt purely literary and artistic aims and the desire to entertain the reader
occupied an important place in the author's mind." Moreover
the work was designed as teaching material, that is, didactic
literature, written from the same perspective as Wisdom literature (Whybray, 1968:13). The problems with such an approach,
where historicity, perspective (wisdom), narrativity (novel), and
semantic function (teaching) are mixed, are clear. How could
any reader possibly know exactly what the story means or what
it refers to?

At the other end of the spectrum are the views of Gunn. He
acknowledges the historicity of persons and events, but nevertheless regards the story of king David as ". . . entertainment which
demands the active engagement of those entertained, which chal-
lenges their intellect, their emotions, their understanding of people, of society and of themselves" (Gunn, 1978:61). According to
him (1978:61) the narrative is not fiction in the sense of "frei
erfunden," although it is possible—as in the case of Icelandic
stories—". . .to detect demonstrably fictitious or highly conventional elements in the stories." From this perspective the *Succession Narrative* is to be read as a story, for example, a historical
novel, as remade reality. The semantic function of the text is non-
descriptive, that is, social, expressive, and instrumental.

It is already becoming clear that an adequate reading of our
embedded parable of Nathan and its application would very
much depend on one's views about the macrotext into which it is
embedded. If it is regarded as history writing, meaning and
reference would be construed in terms of description. Other
views on the text type will equally influence one's reception of
the text. It needs to be said further, however, that the shift from
considering it history writing to political propaganda and

beyond is an indication that scholars are taking increasingly seriously the narrative character of the story of king David.

The history of the reception of Nathan's parable and its
application is equally interesting. The relationship between the
parable and its literary context in 2 Samuel has given rise to
many different readings of the text. Since the days of Schwally
and Gunkel, serious objections have been raised (among others)
about the authenticity of this David story in view of the so-
called incompatibility between the parable of Nathan and its
application in 2 Samuel 12. According to Schwally, it is hardly
possible to reconcile David's struggle for the life of the son of
Bathsheba with his sentence on the man who stole the lamb
from the poor man in the story of Nathan. Moreover, he also
finds it difficult to accept both the image of Nathan as the
prophet who rebukes the king for his affair with Uriah's wife
and the later picture of him (1 Kgs 1) in his involvement to
secure the succession of Bathsheba's second son to the throne of
David as images of the same man (cf. Simon, 1967:208). These
two observations, as well as attempts to reconstruct "what actually happened," ruled the scene of interpretation of the story of
Nathan and David for a very long time.

Various solutions to the problem of the relationship between
Nathan's parable and its application have been offered, ranging
from hypothetical interpolations to detailed discussions of the
possible juridical background of the story told. In all these readings the reconstruction of the events which are not told ("What
actually happened") plays a very important role.

> Our chapter contains no answer to the questions that
> deeply interest us. Had anyone of the court divulged to
> Uriah what had transpired between his wife and the
> king? Can we possibly attribute to him any deliberate
> intention to fail the king's designs and interpret his
> words as a daring protest against the injustice per-
> petrated against him? (Simon, 1967:21)

According to Garsiel (1976:24): ". . . the Bible has apparently failed to elucidate . . ." problems such as: "To what extent
was Bathsheba herself responsible for David's affair with her?
Did Uriah know about her adultery? Exactly how was the murder of Uriah accomplished?" These matters undoubtedly play a
role in how the reference of the text is construed.

Two recent attempts to explain the relationship between the

parable and its context focused on the juridical character of the parable. According to Simon there are five examples of juridical parables in the Old Testament (2 Sam 12:1–14, 14:1–20; 1 Kgs 20:35–43; Isa 5:1–7; and Jer 3:1–5). His definition of a juridical parable is most revealing:

> The juridical parable constitutes a *realistic* story about a violation of the law, related to someone who had committed a similar offence with the purpose of leading the unsuspecting hearer to pass judgement on himself. The offender will only be caught in the trap set for him if he truly believes that the story told him *actually happened* and only if he does not detect prematurely the similarity between the offence in the story and the one he himself has committed. . . . The realistic dress of the juridical parable, on the other hand, is intended to conceal the very fact that it is a parable. (Simon, 1967:220–21; italics mine)

The description is influenced by Simon's interpretation of the application of the parable. It does not offer us a description of what a "juridical" parable is, but tells us for what purposes such a story may be used. As a consequence he presumes that the story (juridical parable) describes a "real legal problem," and that it should be read in view of *that* problem. The metaphorical nature of the text type parable is replaced by a so-called "realistic story" character of the juridical parable, in order to mislead the person who is guilty of the transgression to which the parable refers. This conclusion is doubtful. These parables are not ambiguous in the sense that they can be read both as stories and as reports of what had actually happened. Because the reader is, on the one hand, unaware of the reason why the parable is being told, and, on the other, being presented as a reader (hearer) who reads stories as reports (description), communication fails. Simon's definition of a juridical parable invites the reader to look for certain information in the text which in the end he will also find. This is seen best in the analyses of both Simon and Seebass (1974): ". . . Nathan's story should be examined for traces of a real legal problem justifying its being brought by a third party (the prophet) to the notice of the king" (Simon 1967:226). In this way juridical problems are imposed in the story. According to Seebass (1974:203) there are two irritating juridical problems involved in 2 Samuel 12:1–15: Does the

transgression which is narrated in the parable (theft) justify the
death sentence (cf. v 5)? How can David be forgiven (juridi-
cally) for what he had done by simply pleading guilty (cf. v 13:
"I have sinned against the *Lord*")? By reading these two questions into the text he concludes that the parable told by Nathan
only corresponds to David's transgression if the case intended is
not one of theft but of the exploitation of superior force against
the poor. "On this basis v. 11f. are original, v. 13 a frank acceptance of the verdict, and v. 14 the preservation of the legal
rights of Uriah" (Seebasss, 1974:211). Admittedly this reading of
the parable and its application offers solutions to the *supposed*
incompatibility between the parable and its context in 2 Samuel.
But does it really take the story in 2 Samuel seriously? The narrator of the Nathan and David story in 2 Samuel had no interest,
as far as I can see, in the two problems posed by Seebass. Neither did he want to inform the reader about all the missing data
which scholars like Garsiel and others find so important. By
imposing these problems on the text, the text is read through a
filter which makes it refer to and mean accordingly—be it a
filter of Solomonic dating, deuteronomistic morality, or whatever
the case may be. It should also be noted that in these attempts to
construct the meaning of the text by filling in "missing" data or
making it refer to a "real legal problem," a reader-expectation is
created which need not necessarily be that of the text but rather
that of an enriched text.

Let us now turn to Lategan's reception of the parable and its
application (cf. p. 81). According to him it is the story character
of Nathan's parable that puts David at ease. It causes him to
identify with a fictive character, however incorrectly, because he
sees this poor man as a man of flesh and blood. He is taken by
surprise when he is told that he is the man who took the poor
man's lamb.

> It is important to notice that the embedded story of the
> rich man and the poor man, which forms a perfectly
> self-contained unit on its own, only functions in this
> context beause of the tacit identification of David with
> the rich man. Without this 'outside' reference, the ten-
> sion created by the parable would not exist and the
> point missed.

He denies the fact that parables as stories refer immanently.
He insists that they refer to the outside world by virtue of the

fact that this particular parable refers to David: ". . . because they presuppose a wider referential context, parables become one of the most effective vehicles of redescription."

Apparently Lategan did not notice that we here have an ideal model of reader-response and expectation related to text type. According to our narrator, David did not hear the parable as parable at all. It is therefore not correct to think that the story character of Nathan's parable put David at ease and that as story (second order reference) it opened the possibility for David to step outside his first order context, that is, his literal real world situation. Incidently, David heard the parable as a *description* of what actually happened (first order reference). He identified with the poor man because he regarded him as the victim of exploitation. Is the so-called "identification" of David as "the man" an indication of how parables refer to the outside world? Certainly not. Because the parable is used to say something about somebody, its meaning is referred to by a comparable meaning in the events of the narrated world of king David. What he has done according to our narration is compared to what somebody has done in the fictitious world of the parable. The parable is applied and, because of the application, there is a relationship of reference between text and application. One should furthermore also note that it is not the historical David who is said to be "the man" of the parable but the narrated David. This observation is not without importance, as I will argue below. In its application, the parable indeed has an out-side reference. It is used to say something about somebody (the narrated David) in the narrative world of the text into which it is embedded. It is only in this sense that it is used as a re-description of reality—to use Ricoeur's term—to help redescribe the reality of the narrated David.

In his attempt to apply and defend Ricoeur's theory of re-description as reference in front of the text, Lategan misread the story of Nathan and its application. The semantic function of the parable of Nathan is directly related to its application in the story of David not because parables ". . . presuppose a wider referential context," but because they can be used to say something about somebody or something.

This short survey of a few readings of our text as embedded into the *Succession Narrative* clearly indicates that, despite universal agreement on the narrative character of 2 Samuel, the story is not read as story. It is also clear that historical interests dominate most readings of the text, not, in the sense of seeing the text as part of a specific historical period but rather as referring to historical events and persons. As we have seen, it is argued that even the parable of Nathan refers to some real legal problem or to the historical David.

In the next section reader-response, redescription, and reference will be discussed in view of this thesis and with regard to 2 Samuel 12:1–15.

Reception, Redescription, and Reference

It is unfortunate that reference is too often used in theological literature in connection with the historicity of events and persons mentioned in biblical texts. In this way a semantic problem (reference) is changed into a historical one (historicity) and the problems of text semantics are neglected.

In view of the difference of opinion among scholars about the exact nature of *reference* and Ricoeur's views on *redescription* as a particular kind of reference to reality, which play such · an important role in Lategan's discussions above, it seems necessary to return to the problem again.

The difference between *endophoric* and *exophoric* use of reference items in language communication appears to be basic to the interpretation of texts. In any discourse, reference to something which has already been mentioned or will be mentioned is necessary (cf. Halliday and Hasan, 1976:305). Consider the sentence: "The following morning David wrote a letter to Joab and sent Uriah with it" (2 Sam 12:14). The endophoric use of the items "following morning" and "it" is clear. "Following morning" should be interpreted with reference to the previous evening mentioned in 2 Samuel 12:13 and "it" with reference to "letter" in the same sentence. The co-text (context), that is, the preceding statements as well as what follows, are instructive for construing the meanings of these items. Do these items, however, also refer to extralinguistic referents in the world outside the text? Does the situation in which the communication took place also constitute the meaning of items in the sentence? Are they, in other words, also exophoric? A clearcut answer is not easy, since the existents and events in this sentence are first of all *narrated* existents and events. Even David and Uriah are in the first instance the narrated David and the narrated Uriah. Some would undoubtedly argue that David, and perhaps also Uriah, refer to the David and Uriah who happened to live in Israel long ago. But are these extralinguistic referents constitutive in constructing the meaning of this language communication? I will come back to this below.

Let us now look at another example. In 1 Corinthians 3:1–2 Paul says: "For my part, my brothers, I could not speak to you as I should speak to people who have the Spirit. I had to deal with you on the merely natural plane, as infants in Christ." The use of reference in these sentences is clearly exophoric. "I" refers to "Paul" of flesh and blood and "you" to "those out there in Corinth." Both persons and events point to extralinguistic referents in the first place. Not that the endophoric use of reference items in this kind of statement is denied. However, it is the *situational context* that is constitutive for constructing the meaning in these utterances. In fact, the interpretation of reference items in statements like these depends on situational information, while the interpretation of those mentioned in the previous example depends on the information of the co-text. Text type seems to have a great influence on the referential status of utterances. These two very simple examples, one of which comes from a narrative text and the other forming part of an argumentation, sufficiently illustrate the complicated nature of reference. Not only are there different kinds of reference, but reference also depends on the *nature* of the communication act (narration, exposition, argument, description, listing: cf. Brooks and Warren, 1970:56–57; Nida, 1981:29–30), its context, and the situation in which it happens. "Reference . . . is a context-dependent aspect of utterance meaning" (Lyons, 1981:220).

The relational aspect of reference is made clear by the following remarks by Lyons. He asserts that reference is: ". . . the relation that holds between *linguistic expressions* and what they stand for in the world, or universe of discourse . . ." and that ". . . it is a relation that holds between speakers (more generally, locutionary agents) and what they are talking about on particular occasions" (Lyons, 1981:220). The first of these remarks could be interpreted in terms of Halliday and Hasan's application of exophoric and endophoric use of reference, the importance of which we have already noted. In the second remark we are closer to the problems involved in Lategan's relating of reference to reception. In this

case referance is defined within the framework of a language communication act, where speaker and receptor are involved in construing "what they are talking about." Both parties play an active
role in the construction of reference; the speaker by using "some
appropriate expression" (Lyons, 1977:177) and the receptor by
actively decoding what the speaker attempts to communicate.
Obviously communication will fail or be distorted when the cod-
ing or decoding is done inadequately. For instance, when a
speaker's narrative is read as description there would be a dis-
agreement between "what they (= speaker and receptor) are
talking about." This has been illustrated above with a survey of
receptions of the *Succession Narrative*. Two things should be
noted. In order to communicate properly both speaker and receptor should be in agreement in their construing of "what they are
talking about." Secondly, "what they are talking about" is a semantic phenomenon. In view of this, let us return to my thesis about
semantic function and reference.

The distinction between the different semantic functions of
the same or different units of language, like phrases or sentences,
has far-reaching implications for our present discussion and also
for the interpretation of texts. In the words of Lyons (1977:50):

> Many semanticists have talked as if language was used
> solely, or primarily, for the communication of factual
> information. Others have maintained that making state-
> ments descriptive of states-of-affairs is but one of the
> functions of language; that it also serves, as do our other
> customs and patterns of behaviour, for the establishment
> and maintenance of social relationships and for the
> expression of our personality.

Undoubtedly not all statements in biblical texts have the
semantic function of communicating "factual information," that
is, of being descriptive. Think of admonitions, miracle stories,
parables, and other kinds of statements which function semantically in a non-descriptive way. In Mark's Gospel, for example,
the miracle stories are used (semantically) to characterize Jesus
and his opponents.

Seen from the perspective of the so-called speech-act theory
(cf. Chatman, 1978:161–66), the same sentence may be used for
different meanings in accordance with the speech act which is
performed. The same sentence may be uttered as an assertion, a

warning, a prediction, a promise, a threat, or whatever illocutionary act involved. This would obviously influence both the
meaning and the reference of such an utterance.

Because the semantic function of sentences may be descriptive or non-descriptive, and because different speech acts may
be involved in performing the same sentence, it is absolutely
necessary that speaker and receptor have to know exactly "what
they are talking about." This also holds for written communication. The fact that different text types (narration, exposition,
argument, description, and listing) do not necessarily refer in the
same way as far as exophoric reference is concerned also has
important implications for our discussion. This is where
Ricoeur's theory of *redescription* comes into the picture in connection with non-descriptive texts like narratives.

In my chapter on the parables of Jesus above, I have argued
that Ricoeur is not addressing the problem of *what the speaker
and receptor are talking about* (reference) in the case of metaphors and parables, but about what they *are*, that is, a remaking
of the world (cf. above). In his attempt to break with the idea
that narratives refer immanently to the reality of a narrative
world, Ricoeur concerns himself with what a narrative achieves.
According to him, narratives reshape reality; they refer in front
of the text (cf. Ricoeur, 1979:124). His distinction between *productive* and *reproductive* reference in connection with fiction is
useful insofar as it clearly distinguishes descriptive from non-
descriptive language usage. In fiction, reality is present not in a
reproduced sense of a given original (the existing thing) outside
the text to which it could be referred. Fiction produces reality,
and therefore *absence* (of an original) and *unreality* should not
be confused. Unlike a photograph, where the original is absent,
fiction produces reality by combining components ". . . derived
from previous experience" (Ricoeur, 1979:125). The original is
not reproduced. "Writing a poem, telling a story, construing an
hypothesis, a plan, or a strategy: these are kinds of contexts of
work which provide a perspective to imagination and allow it to
be 'productive'" (Ricoeur, 1979:125). This also holds for metaphors, which are very good examples of redescription of reality
because they are semantic innovations. His remarks about
fifteenth-century Flemish painters illuminate his understanding
of redescription.

> Painting, with them, remains mimetic in the sense that
> aspects of the reality are restored, but painting only
> reaches its goal under the condition of inventing the
> medium of that mimesis. Ever since, imitation is no
> longer a reduplication of reality but a creative rendering
> of it. (Ricoeur, 1979:138)

The same holds for poetry, which is also a redescription of
reality. Up to this point Ricoeur is clear, but to my mind a shift
then takes place between what a fiction (painting, metaphor
etc.) *is*, and what a fiction does (can do). This difference is best
illustrated by the following remark about models and fiction:

> Models in turn provide us with the more accurate
> account of what we have attempted to describe as pro-
> ductive reference. To the extent that models are not
> models *of* . . . i.e., still pictures of a previously given
> reality, *but models for*, i.e., heuristic fictions for re-
> describing reality, the work of the model becomes in
> turn a model for construing in a meaningful way the
> concept of the productive reference of all fictions,
> including the so-called poetic fictions. (Ricoeur, 1979:
> 140–41; italics mine)

He simply asserts, without substantiation, that a fiction *is* a
redescription as well as a redescription *for*. With this in mind, it
is difficult to relate productive reference—which is the name for
the creative and non-descriptive semantic function of "fictions"—to reference *in front of the text*. By remaking reality, be
it in a narrative, metaphor, painting, or whatever other "fiction,"
a text is created of which the meaning has to be decoded. Peak
communication will only be possible if the receptor is able to
construe the meaning of what the sender is talking about in his
redescription of reality. In the end productive reference appears
to be the network of reference (for example, the narrative world
of a story) which is created by writers of poems, story-tellers, et
cetera when they redescribe reality by means of new combina-
tions (of existing and non-existing things).

The problem with Ricoeur's view on redescription is that
they are too inclusive. He wants both to explain and also to create reality, and uses the term "productive reference" for both
activities. That is one of the reasons why Lategan's application
of the concept of redescription to the growth and communication of biblical texts is problematic. The possibilities which texts

create do not depend on reference in front of but on the making of new texts.

With this in mind, let us now consider again the parable of Nathan and its application in 2 Samuel. It has, to my mind, been adequately indicated that the *Succession Narrative* is a *story* (cf. Gunn, 1978, and Bar-Efrat, 1978). This I will not—except for a few necessary remarks below— argue any further. It follows, however, that if 2 Samuel 12:1–14 is embedded into a narrative, it should also be read as part of that narrative.

The story of David, Uriah, and Bathsheba is told at a crucial point in the development of the plot of the story of king David. In 2 Samuel vv 11–12, a complication takes place in the plot when David ironically attempts to *take* the wife of Uriah by force. Unlike the previous section, where David is presented as a king content to be *given* a kingdom by Yahweh (cf. 2 Sam vv 2–5), he is now presented as a keen schemer who does everything possible to seize a wife for himself (cf. Gunn, 1978:97). The episode gives the pattern of intrigue, sex, and violence in a nutshell which ". . . is played out at length in the subsequent story within David's own family" (Gunn, 1978:98). This violent seizure of Uriah's wife is not accepted by Yahweh without serious consequences for his kingdom (2 Sam 12:8–11). Gunn (1978:98) is correct when he says: "However precisely one interprets Nathan's parable in relation to its setting . . . it is absolutely plain that it encapsulates the essence of David's dealing with Bathsheba, the episode is the story of the rich man who *took* the poor man's lamb." The story and its application is used to characterize David by the application of various narrative techniques including irony. Irony is a very effective device for for steering the reception of the text. It is often used to develop characterization and to set norms of judgement for the reader. I · have already referred to the ironic contrast between David being given a kingdom and his attempt to seize a wife. The tension between retribution and forgiveness, which is not absolutely solved in the story, is heightened by the ironic treatment of David in connection with the death of Uriah. Even Yahweh's role in the story ". . . retains a measure of ambivalence if not an undercurrent of irony" (Gunn, 1978:98). Because of his faithfulness to his principles and his king, Uriah ironically brings about his own death. He even unwittingly carries out his own death sentence. David ironically passes judgement upon himself after hearing the parable of Nathan. Bar-Efrat (1978:22) remarks correctly: "Often the irony serves to express criticism of the characters concerned in an implicit and indirect way." This is exactly the purpose of irony in the David, Uriah, and Bathsheba story, which is told primarily to characterize David the king.

Speeches and actions are also very important aspects of characterization. They provide the reader with information about narrated figures and how the sender wants the receptor to see them. This is particularly true of the story of David and Bathsheba. Notice how the characters are presented to the reader through the eyes of the narrated David and *not* through the eyes of Bathsheba. How he sees and meets the characters is narrated. This is part of the way in which David is shaped for the audience (receptors). In the end the reader either identifies or rejects the character because of his characterization. In an almost matter-of-fact manner David is presented as a deviser of plans in order to take the wife of Uriah. If the plan does not work out, the next is implemented. In the end, he succeeds at the cost of the life of Uriah. But this success is a failure, however, since he pronounces himself guilty by misinterpreting the parable of Nathan. The flow and development of the story (*Succession Narrative*) is made possible by this reaction to Nathan's story. In short, a reading of the story of David which does not take seriously the narrative character of 2 Samuel is bound to distort the communication between text and reader. 2 Samuel clearly is a redescription of reality. It is not a reproduction or a replica. It invites the reader to participate in a network of significances created by a combination of events and people. The function of the story is *non-descriptive* in the above sense of the term.

Semantic Function and Reference

Let us now consider again Nathan's parable and its application with a view to reception, redescription, and reference in the light of the thesis of this essay.

The semantic function of the statement "You are the man" should be read with reference to its context. It forms part of a narrative and has the function of pointing back to the *narrative world* of an embedded narrative. This embedded narrative (Nathan's parable) is used in 2 Samuel to characterize David negatively. His character is shaped by the story of Nathan as well as by his reception thereof. To the reader, however, he is presented as acceptable again by his confession of guilt. It is not possible to read the sentence "You are the man" as an ontological statement about the "real" David who used to be king of Israel; neither does it refer outside the main narrative world of 2 Samuel to the real world; David is also not identified as *the man*. The narrated David is told that, by taking Uriah's wife, he acted the role of the character who took the poor man's lamb in Nathan's parable. Ricoeur's distinction (1978b:248) between two functions of "to be" is helpful in this respect. On some occasions "is" is used to denote equivalence, but "is" can also be used as a simile, "to be like." The actions of David are to be compared to those of the man in Nathan's story: David is like . . . or acted like. . . . The following remarks of Halliday and Hasan are equally illuminating:

> Either the reference item is interpreted through being IDENTIFIED with the referent in question; or it is interpreted through being COMPARED with the referent. . . . (1976:309)

> Comparison differs from the other forms of reference in that it is based not on identity of reference but on non-identity: the reference item is interpreted, not by being identified with what it presupposes, but by being compared with it. (1976:313)

Notice that in our sentence the reference item *you* (David), is *compared* to a character in Nathan's story and not vice versa. It is not the story of Nathan as such that refers to an outside referent in 2 Samuel 12. In its application a character outside the story is compared with a character in the story. Because of its application to a particular situation in the narrative world of 2 Samuel, the story of Nathan, like that of the Good Samaritan in Luke, has a performative semantic function. It denounces the action of a narrated figure and characterizes him negatively. It also is an anticipation of David's confession of guilt and makes clear what this confession refers to.

Nathan's story is, like any other parable, a self-contained unit. It can stand on its own and has a meaning of its own. It is a complete story with plot, characters, and point of view. Like the parables of Jesus, it can, however, be used in different contexts with different meanings and for different purposes.

In our context it is used for a very specific purpose which also determines its semantic function. The fact that David read the story as a report, while Nathan intended it as a story about David's handling of his affair with Uriah's wife, explains the lack of communication between David and Nathan and also tells the reader how to read it. The modern reader might miss quite a bit of the subtle information embedded into the context of Nathan's story which the ancient reader would have enjoyed. In his recent article Peter Coxon (1981), for example, draws attention to the fact that in chapter 11 David is the agent on four occasions of *šlḥ* in his manipulation of the situation. In chapter 12 it is Yahweh, however, who sends Nathan to David to rebuke him. The terminology used by Uriah to reject David's encouragement to enjoy conjugal rights with his wife also appears in Nathan's story (cf. "eat," "drink," and "to lie with"). "Ancient audiences would have relished the thick irony which laces the narrator's account of the ewe lamb in the next chapter when the same terminology reappears" (Coxon, 1981:249). Suffice it to say that the repetition of terminology, with its ironic effect, adds to the fact that 2 Samuel is a network of internal reference.

The relationship between the parable of Nathan and its application can only be properly understood if the context within which it occurs is taken seriously. This context is a narrative. If it is taken into account that the parable is used to say something about the narrated David of 2 Samuel, and how crucial the episode of David, Uriah, and Bathsheba is for the development of the plot, the comparison of the narrated David to the rich man will be the focal point in a search for what it refers to. The semantic function of the story—that is, characterization—determines its reference and referential status. The story of Nathan in 2 Samuel does not refer to some "real legal problem," as Seebass and others would think, but is used like the story of the Tekoite woman to characterize David as a man who was too clever by half. The norms of judgment of his action are given in the text. "Nathan the prophet denounces David's behaviour concerning Bathsheba and Uriah, and David himself confesses his guilt. . . . His confession demonstrates, for all his misdemeanor, his moral greatness" (Bar-Efrat, 1978:24). The reception of the text is determined by its text type and so is the semantic function and reference.

Bibliography

Abrams, M. H.
1971   *A Glossary of Literary Terms.* 3d ed. New York: Harry Holt.

Bar-Efrat, S.
1978   "Literary Modes and Methods in the Biblical Narrative in View of 2 Samuel 10–20 and 1 Kings 1–2." *Immanuel* 8:19–31.

Barr, D. L.
1977   *Toward a Definition of the Gospel Genre: A Generic Analysis and Comparison of the Synoptic Gospels and the Socratic Dialogues by Means of Aristotle's Theory of Tragedy.* Ann Arbor: University Microfilms. Ph.D. diss., Florida State University, 1974.

Bartholomäus, W.
1974   *Kleine Predigtlehre.* Köln: Benziger.

Beardslee, W. A.
1970   *Literary Criticism of the New Testament.* Philadelphia: Fortress Press.

Beker, J. C.
1980   *Paul the Apostle.* Philadelphia: Fortress Press.

Best, E.
1977   "The Role of the Disciples in Mark." *NTS* 23: 377–401.

Betz, H-D.
1979   *Galatians: A Commentary on Paul's Letters to the Churches in Galatia.* Philadelphia: Fortress Press.

Blumenberg, H.
1961   "Wirklichkeitsbegriff und Möglichkeit des Romans." Pp. 9–27 in *Nachahmung und Illusion.* Ed. H. R. Jauss. Munich: Fink.

Boomershine, T. E.
1974   *Mark, the Storyteller: A Rhetorical-Critical Investigation of Mark's Passion and Resurrection Narrative.* New York: Union Theological Seminary.

Booth, W. C.
1961   *The Rhetoric of Fiction.* Chicago: University of Chicago Press.

Brooks, C., and Warren, R. P.
1970   *Modern Rhetoric.* 3d ed. New York: Harcourt Brace.

Bürger P.
    1977   "Rezeptionsästhetik—Zwischenbalanz (III): Pro-
                bleme der Rezeptionsforschung." *Poetica* 9: 446–71.
Caird, G. B.
    1980   *The Language and Imagery of the Bible.* Philadel-
                phia: Westminster Press.
Carlston, C. E.
    1975   *The Parables of the Triple Tradition.* Philadelphia:
                Fortress Press.
Chatman, S.
    1978   *Story and Discourse: Narrative Structure in Fiction
                and Film.* Ithaca: Cornell University Press.
Coxon, P. W.
    1981   "A Note on 'Bathsheba' in 2 Samuel 12:1–6." *Bib* 62:
                247–50.
Crossan, J. D.
    1976   "Parable, Allegory and Paradox." Pp. 267–318 in
                *Exploration of the Possibilities Offered by Structural-
                ism for Exegesis.* Ed. D. Patte. Pittsburgh: Pickwick.
    1979   *Finding is the First Act: Trove Folktales and Jesus'
                Treasure Parable.* Missoula, MT: Scholars Press/Phila-
                delphia: Fortress Press.
    1979/80   "Paradox Gives Rise to Metaphor: Paul Ricoeur's Her-
                meneutics and the Parables of Jesus." *BR* 24/25: 20–37.
    1980   *Cliffs of Fall: Paradox and Polyvalence in the Parables
                of Jesus.* New York: Seabury.
Delekat, L.
    1967   "Tendenz und Theologie der David-Salomo-Erzäh-
                lung." Pp. 26–36 in *Das ferne und nahe Wort.* Ed. F.
                Maas. BZAW 105. Berlin: Töpelmann.
Delorme, J., ed.
    1979   *Zeichen und Gleichnisse: Evangelientext und semi-
                otische Forschung.* Düsseldorf: Patmos.
Dodd, C. H.
    1936   *The Parables of the Kingdom.* Welwyn: Nisbet.
Dorsch, T. S.
    1965   *Classical Literary Criticism.* Harmondsworth: Pen-
                guin.
Dressler, W.
    1973   *Einführung in die Textlinguistik.* 2d ed. Tübingen:
                Niemeyer.
Du Plessis, I. J.
    1980   "Realiteit en Interpretasie in die Nuwe Testament."
                Theologia Evangelica 13:25–41.
Eco, U.
    1972   *Einführung in die semiotik.* Uni-Taschenbücher 105.
                Munich: Fink.

1977   *Zeichen*. Frankfurt: Suhrkamp.
1979   *The Role of the Reader: Explorations in the Semiotics of Texts*. Bloomington: Indiana University Press.

Enzenberger, C.
1981   "Die Grenze der literarischen Utopie." *Akzente* 1:44–60

Finkel, A.
1964   *The Pharisees and the Teacher of Nazareth: A Study on their Background, their Halachic and Midrashic Teachings, the Similarities and Differences*. Leiden: E. J. Brill.

Foder, J. D.
1977   *Semantics: Theories of Meaning in Generative Grammar*. Sussex: Spires.

Frankemölle, H.
1982   "Kommunikatives Handeln in Gleichnissen Jesu: Historischkritische und pragmatische Exegese. Eine kritische Sichtung." *NTS* 28: 61–90.

Frey, E.
1974   "Rezeption literarischer Stilmittel." *Zeitschrift für Literaturwissenschaft und Linguistik* 4:80–94.

Frey, G.
1970   "Hermeneutische und hypothetischdeduktive Methode." *Zeitschrift für allgemeine Wissenschaftstheorie* 1:35–40.

Funk, R. W.
1966   *Language, Hermeneutic, and Word of God: The Problem of Language in the New Testament and Contemporary Theology*. New York: Harper & Row.

Gadamer, H-G.
1975   *Wahrheit und Methode*. 4th ed. Tübingen: Mohr.

Garland, D. E.
1979   *The Intention of Matthew 23*. Novum Testamentum Supplements 52. Leiden: E. J. Brill

Garsiel, M.
1976   "David and Bathsheba." I, II & III. *Dor le Dor* 5: 24–28, 85–90, 134–37.

Genette, G.
1980   *Narrative discourse*. Oxford: Blackwell.

Gnilka, J.
1979   *Das Evangelium nach Markus (MK 1–8, 26)*. EKKNT II/2 Zürich: Benziger.

Goodman, N.
1965   *Fact, Fiction and Forecast*. 2d ed. Indianapolis: Bobbs-Merrill Co.

1966   *The Structure of Appearance*. 2d ed. Indianapolis: Bobbs-Merrill Co.

1968   *Languages of Art: An Approach to a Theory of Symbols.* Indianapolis: Bobbs-Merrill Co.
1969   *Languages of Art.* London: Oxford University Press.
1978   *Ways of Worldmaking.* Sussex: Harvester.
1981   "Wege der Referenz." *Zeitschrift für Semiotik* 3: 11–22.

Grimm, G.
1975   *Literatur and Lesen.* Stuttgart: Reclam.
1977   "Receptionsgeschichte: Prämissen und Möglichkeiten historischer Darstellung." Pp. 144–86 in *Internationales Archiv fur Sozialgeschichte der deutschen Literatur,* vol 2. Eds. G. Jäger, A. Martino, and F. Sengle. Tübingen: Niemeyer.

Guillaumont, A., et al.
1959   *Het Evangelie naar de Beschrijving van Thomas.* Coptic text and translation by A. Guillaumont, et al. Leiden: E. J. Brill.

Gunn, D. M.
1978   *The Story of King David; Genre and Interpretation.* Journal for the Study of the Old Testament. Supplement Series, 6. Sheffield: University of Sheffield, Department of Biblical Studies.

Güttgemanns, E.
1971a   "Die linguistisch-didaktische Methodik der Gleichnisse Jesu." Pp. 99–183 in *Studia Linguistica Neotestamentica: Gesammelte Aufsätze zur linguistischen Grundlage einer Neutestamentlichen Theologie.* Ed. E. Güttgemanns. BEvT 60. Munich: Kaiser.
1971b   *Offene Fragen zur Formgeschichte des Evangeliums.* 2d ed. BEvT 54. Munich: Kaiser.
1978   *Einführung in die Linguistik für Textwissenschaftler.* Bonn: Linguistica Biblica.

Haenchen, E.
1951   "Matthaus 23." *ZThK* 48: 38–62.

Halliday, M. A. K., and Hasan, R.
1976   *Cohesion in English.* London: Longman.

Harnisch W.
1979   "Die Metaphor als heuristisches Prinzip. Neuerscheinungen zur Hermeneutik der Gleichnisreden Jesu." *VF* 24: 53–89.

Hartlich, C.
1980   "Is de historisch-kritische methode achterhaald?" *Concilium* 16: 7–12.

Hernadi, P.
1976   "Literary Theory: A Compass for Critics." *Critical Enquiry* 3: 369–86.

Hohendahl, P. U.
1974   "Einleitung: Zur Lage der Rezeptionsforschung." *Zeitschrift für Literaturwissenschaft und Linguistik* 4: 7–11.

Huffman, N. A.
1978   "Atypical Features in the Parables of Jesus." *JBL* 97: 207–20.

Iser, W.
1974   *The Implied Reader.* Baltimore: John Hopkins University Press.
1976   *Der Akt des Lesens.* Munich: Fink.
1980   Interview with R. E. Keunzli. *Diacritics* (June): 57–74.

Jakobson, R.
1960   "Linguistics and Poetics." Pp. 350–77 in *Style in Language.* Ed. T. A. Sebeok. Cambridge, MA: M.I.T. Press.

Japp, U.
1977   *Hermeneutik: der theoretische Diskurs, die Literatur und die Konstruktion ihres Zusammenhanges in den philologischen Wissenschaften.* Munich: Fink.

Jauss, H.R.
1969   "Paradigmawechsel in der Literaturwissenschaft." *Linguistische Berichte* 3: 44–56.
1974a   "Literary History as a Challenge to Literary Theory." Pp. 11–41 in *New Directions in Literary History.* Ed. R. Cohen. London: John Hopkins University Press.
1974b   *Literaturgeschichte als Provokation.* 5th ed. Frankfurt: Suhrkamp.
1975   "Der Leser als Instanz einer neuen Geschichte der Literatur." *Poetica* 7: 325–44.

Jeremias, J.
1970   *Die Gleichnisse Jesu.* 8th ed. Göttingen: Vandenhoeck & Ruprecht.

Jülicher, A.
1963   *Die Gleichnisreden Jesu.* Darmstadt: Wisenschaftliche Buchgesellschaft.

Jüngel, E.
1962   *Paulus und Jesus.* Tübingen: Mohr.
1969   "Die Welt als Möglichkeit und Wirklichkeit: Zum ontologischen Ansatz der Rechtfertigungslehre." *EvTh* 29: 417–42.
1978   *Gott als Geheimnis der Welt: Zur Begründung der Theologie des Gekreuzigten im Streit zwischen Theismus und Atheismus.* 3d ed. Tübingen: Mohr.

Kelber, W. H.
    1974   *The Kingdom in Mark: A New Place and a New Time.*
                Philadelphia: Fortress Press.

Kempson, R. M.
    1977   *Semantic Theory.* Cambridge: Cambridge University
                Press.

Kermode, F.
    1979   *The Genesis of Secrecy.* Cambridge, MA: Harvard
                University Press.

Kingsbury, J.D.
    1972   "The Parables of Jesus in Current Research." *Dialog*
                11: 101–7.
    1981   "The 'Divine Man' as the Key to Mark's Christology:
                The end of an era?" *Int* 35: 243–57.

Kissinger, W. S.
    1979   *The Parables of Jesus: A History of Intrepretation and
                Bibliography.* ATLA Bibliography Series 4. Metu-
                chen: Scarecrow.

Kosselleck, R.
    1973   "Ereignis und Struktur." Pp. 560–71 in *Geschichte-
                Ereignis und Erzählung.* Ed. R. Koselleck and W-D.
                Stempel. Munich: Fink.

Kuhn, H-W.
    1971   *Ältere Sammlungen im Markusevangelium. SUNT 8.*
                8 Göttingen: Vandenhoeck & Ruprecht.

Kümmel, W. G.
    1982   "Ein Jahrhundert Erforschung der Eschatologie des
                Neuen Testaments." *TLZ* 107: 81–96.

Lambrecht, J.
    1969   *Marcus Interpretator: Stijl en Boodschap in Mc.
                3:20–24, 34.* Brugge: Desclée de Brouwer.

Lategan, B.C.
    1973   "Tradition and Interpretation: Two Methodological
                Remarks." *Neotestamentica* 7: 95–103.
    1977   "Structural Interrelations in Matthew 11–12." *Neotes-
                tamentica* 11: 115–29.
    1978a   "Het Motief van de Dienst in Galaten 1 en 2." Pp.
                76–84 in *De Knechtsgestalte van Christus.* Ed. H. H.
                Grosheide, et al. Kampen: Kok.
    1978b   "Structural Analysis as Basis for Further Exegetical
                Procedures." Pp. 341–60 in *Society of Biblical Litera-
                ture 1978 Seminar Papers* I. Ed. P. J. Achtemeier. Mis-
                soula, MT: Scholars Press.
    1979   "The Historian and the Believer." Pp. 113–34 in *Scrip-
                ture and the Use of Scripture.* Ed. W. S. Vorster. Preto-
                ria: Unisa.

Link, J.
1979   *Literaturwissenschaftliche Grundbegriffe.* 2d ed. Munich: Fink.
Linnemann, E.
1961   *Gleichnisse Jesu: Einführung und Auslegung.* Göttingen: Vandenhoeck & Ruprecht.
Luz, U.
1971   "Die Jünger im Matthäusezangelium." *ZNW* 62:377–414.
Lyons, J.
1977   *Semantics I.* Cambridge: Cambridge University Press.
1981   *Language, Meaning and Context.* London: Fontana.
Maartens, P. J.
1980   "Mark 2:18–22: An Exercise in Theoretically-Founded Exegesis." *Scriptura* 2: 1–54.
Marxsen, W.
1959   *Der Evangelist Markus: Studien zur Redaktionsgeschichte des Evangeliums.* Göttingen: Vandenhoeck & Ruprecht.
McKnight, E. V.
1978   *Meaning in Texts.* Philadelphia: Fortress Press.
Naumann, M., ed.
1975   *Gesellschaft-Literatur-Lesen.* Berlin: Aufbau-Verlag.
1977   "Das Dilemma der 'Rezeptionsästhetik.'" *Weimarer Beiträge* 23: 5–21.
Nida, E. A.
1981   *Signs, Sense, Translation.* Pretoria: University of Pretoria, Department of Greek.
Nida, E. A., et al.
1983   *Style and Discourse: With Special Reference to the Text of the Greek New Testament.* Cape Town: Bible Society of SA.
Palmer, R. E.
1969   *Hermeneutics.* Evanston: Northwestern University Press.
Patte, D., ed.
1976   *Semiology and Parables: Exploration of the Possibilities Offered by Structuralism for Exegesis.* Pittsburgh: Pickwick.
1980   "One Text: Several Structures." *Semeia* 18: 3–22.
Perrin, N.
1971   "The Modern Interpretation of the Parables of Jesus and the Problem of Hermeneutics." *Int* 25: 131–48.
1976   *Jesus and the Language of the Kingdom: Symbol and Metaphor in New Testament Interpretation.* London: SCM.

Pesch, R.
  1976   *Das Markusevangelium.* HTKNT II/I. Freiburg: Herder.
Petersen, N. R.
  1978a   *Literary Criticism for New Testament Critics.* Philadelphia: Fortress Press.
  1978b   "'Point of view' in Mark's narrative." *Semeia* 12:97–121.
Polanyi, L.
  1981a   "Telling the same story twice." *Text* 1: 313–36.
  1981b   "What stories can tell us about their teller's world." *Poetics Today* 2:97–112.
Price, G.
  1982   *Narratology: The Form and Function of Narrative.* Berlin: Mouton.
Ricoeur, P.
  1973   "Sprache und Theologie des Wortes." Pp. 201–21 in *Exegese im Methodenkonflikt.* Ed. X. Léon-Dufour. Munich: Kösel-Verlag.
  1975   "Biblical Hermeneutics." *Semeia* 4: 27–148, esp. 75–106.
  1976   *Interpretation Theory: Discourse and the Surplus of Meaning.* Fort Worth: Texas Christian University Press.
  1978a   "The Narrative Function." *Semeia* 13: 177–202.
  1978b   *The Rule of Metaphor: Multi-disciplinary Studies of the Creation of Meaning in Language.* London: Routledge and Kegan Paul.
  1979   "The Function of Fiction in Shaping Reality." *Man and World* 12: 123–41.
Roussouw, H. W.
  1980   *Wetenskap, Interpretasie, Wysheid.* Port Elizabeth: University of Port Elizabeth.
Rost, L.
  1926   *Die Überlieferung von der Thronnachfolge Davids* BWANT III/6. Stuttgart: Kohlhammer.
Sacks, S., ed.
  1978   *On metaphor.* Chicago: Chicago University Press.
Schmidt, S. J.
  1975   "Reception and Interpretation of Written Texts as Problems of a Rational Theory of Literary Communication." Pp. 339–408 in *Style and Text, studies presented to* N. E. Enkvist. Ed. H. Ringbom. Stockholm: Spraaktoerlaget Skriptor.
  1980   "Fictionality in Literary and Non-Literary Discourse." *Poetics* 9: 525–46

Schmithals, W.
1979   *Das Evangelium nach Markus* 1. Würzburg: Echter.
Scholes, R., and Kellogg, R.
1966   *The Nature of Narrative.* New York: Oxford University
              Press.
Schweizer, E.
1973   *Das Evangelium nach Matthäus.* Das Neue Testament
              Deutsch 2. Göttingen: Vandenhoeck & Ruprecht.
Seebass, H.
1974   "Nathan und David in II Sam 12." *ZAW* 86: 203–11.
Segers, R. T.
1980   *Het Lezen van Literatuur: Een Inleiding tot een
              Nieuwe Literatuurbenadering.* Baarn: Ambo.
Shipley, J. T., ed.
1970   *Dictionary of World Literary Terms.* Boston: The
              Writer.
Simon, U.
1967   "The Poor Man's Ewe-lamb. An Example of a Juridi-
              cal Parable." *Bib* 48: 207–42.
Steinmetz, H.
1975   "Rezeption und Interpretation: Versuch einer Abgren-
              zung." *Amsterdamer Beiträge zur älteren Germanistik*
              3: 37–81.
Stempel, W-D.
1973   "Erzählung, Beschreibung und der Historische Dis-
              kurs." Pp. 325–46 in *Geschichte-Ereignis und
              Erzählung.* Ed. R. Koselleck and W-D. Stempel.
              Munich: Fink.
Strack, H. L, and Billerbeck, P.
1926, 1928   *Kommentar zum Neuen Testament aus Talmud und
              Midrasch.* I, IV. Munich: Beck.
Strawson, P. F.
1971   *Logico-linguistic Papers.* London: Methuen.
Stuhlmacher, P.
1979   *Vom Verstehen des Neuen Testaments.* Göttingen:
              Vandenhoeck and Ruprecht.
Tannehill, R. C.
1977   "The Disciples in Mark: The Function of a Narrative
              Role." *JR* 57: 386–405.
1979   "The Gospel of Mark as Narrative Christology."
              Semeia 16: 57–95.
Te Selle, S. M.
1974   "Parable, Metaphor, and Theology." *JAAR* 42:
              630–45.
Thiselton, A. C.
1980   *The Two Horizons: New Testament Hermeneutics and*

Philosophical Description with Special Reference to Heidegger, Bultmann, Gadamer, and Wittgenstein. Exeter: Paternoster Press.

Tolbert, M. A.
1979   *Perspectives on the Parables: An Approach to Multiple Interpretations.* Philadelphia: Fortress Press.

Traugott, E. C., and Pratt, M. L.
1980   *Linguistics for Students of Literature.* New York: Harcourt and Brace.

Tucker, G. M.
1971   *Form Criticism of the Old Testament.* Philadelphia: Fortress Press.

Van der Merwe, P. P.
1962   "Vers en Simbool: 'n Ondersoek na die Simbool in sy Betrekking tot die Poësie." DPhil thesis, University of Stellenbosch, Stellenbosch.

Vandermoere, H.
1976   *The Study of the Novel: A Structural Approach.* Leuven: Acco.

Van Peursen, C. A.
1972   *Feiten, Waarden, Gebeurtenissen.* Kampen: Kok.

Veijola, T.
1975   *Die Ewige Dynastie: David und die Entstehung seiner Dynastie nach der deuteronomistischen Darstellung.* Helsinki: Suomalainen Tiedeakatemia.

Via, D. O.
1970   *Die Gleichnisse Jesu: Ihre literarische und existentiale Dimension.* BevT 57. München: Kaiser.

Visagie, P. J.
1978   "Die Vraag na die Grondstruktuur." I & II. *Tydskrif vir Christelike Wetenskap* 14: 4–37, 34–59.

Vorster, W. S.
1977   *'n Ou boek in 'n nuwe wêreld.* Pretoria: Unisa.
1980a   "Die Evangelie Volgens Markus: Inleiding en Teologie." Pp. 109–55 in *Die Sinoptiese Evangelies en Handelinge:* Inleiding en Teologie. Ed. A. B. du Toit. Pretoria: NG Kerkboekhandel.
1980b   "Mark: Collector, Redactor, Author, Narrator?" *Journal of Theology for Southern Africa* 31: 46–61.
1980c   "Die Tekssoort Evangelie en Verwysing." *Theologia Evangelica* 13:27–48.
1981a   "The Function of the Use of the Old Testament in Mark." *Neotestamentica* 14:62–72.
1981b   *Wat is 'n Evangelie? Die Plek van die Tekssoort Evangelie in die Literatuurgeskiedenis.* Pretoria: NG Kerkboekhandel.

1982   "Redaction, Contextualization and the Sayings of Jesus." Pp. 491–500 in *Logia: Les Paroles de Jésus—the Sayings of Jesus. Mémorial Joseph Coppens.* Ed. J. Delobel. BETL 59. Leeuven: Peters.

Weder, H.
1978   *Die Gleichnisse Jesu als Metaphern: Traditions- und redaktionsgeschichtliche Analysen und Interpretationen.* Göttingen: Vandenhoeck & Ruprecht.
1980   "Zum Problem einer 'christlichen Exegese.'" *NTS* 27: 64–82.

Weeden, T. J.
1971   *Mark: Traditions in Conflict.* Philadelphia: Fortress Press.
1979   "Recovering the Parabolic Intent in the Parable of the Sower." *JAAR* 47: 97–120.

Wenham, D.
1982   Review article of H. Weder, *Die Gleichnisse Jesus als Metaphern. Traditons-und redaktionsgeschichtliche Analysen und Interpretationen* (Göttingen: Vandenhoeck & Ruprecht [1978], 312 pp.). *JSNT* 14: 119–23.

Whybray, R. N.
1968   *The Succession Narrative.* London: SCM.

Wildekamp, A., van Montfoort, I., and van Ruiswijk, W.
1980   "Fictionality and convention." *Poetics* 9: 547–67.

Wilder, A. N.
1971   *Early Christian Rhetoric: The Language of the Gospel.* Cambridge, MA: Harvard University Press.

Wilmsatt, W. K.
1954   *The Verbal Icon.* Lexington: University of Kentucky Press.

Wittig, S.
1977   "A Theory of Multiple Meanings." *Semeia* 9: 75–103.

Wrede, W.
1969   *Das Messiasgeheimnis in den Evangelien: Zugleich ein Betirag zum Verständnis des Markusevangeliums.* 4th ed. Göttingen: Vandenhoeck & Ruprecht. 1st ed., 1901.

Wuellner, W.
1981   "Narrative Criticism and the Lazarus Story." Paper read at the 1981 meeting of the SNTS in Rome.

Zimmermann, B.
1974   "Der Leser als Produzent: Zur Problematik der rezeptionsästhetischen Methode." *Zeitschrift für Literaturwissenschaft und Linguistik* 4: 12–26.